MIDDLE CLASS

⬇⬇ TO ⬇⬇

MULTI-MILLIONAIRE

HOW I DID IT THROUGH REAL ESTATE BEFORE 30 AND HOW YOU CAN TOO!

KYLE KOVATS

KOVCO Publications 80 West Century Road,
Suite B22 Paramus, NJ 07652

KOVCO Publications Edition January 2021

Print ISBN : 978-1-09836-443-4

MIDDLE CLASS TO MULTI-MILLIONAIRE

Mom,

I truly do not know where I'd be today without you. All the sacrifices you made for me and Kristi as a single parent growing up did not go unnoticed. Now, in my 30's I look back in hindsight and can't help but imagine where I'd be without you.

TABLE OF CONTENTS

PREFACE

March 22, 2020. The country has been shut down for a week now since the coronavirus has exploded in the US. I'm laying in bed in my studio apartment in Hoboken, NJ and beginning to think, "what if this event wipes out all I've worked for in my life? Could I bounce back and grow it from scratch again?" The answer is of course, yes, but where would I start? I go on Airbnb and book a cabin in the Great Smoky Mountains for the following day and go hiking for a week, by myself. Screw it, just do it, right? I've lived by this mantra my whole life, why stop now?

While hiking that week, I did a lot of soul searching and came to the realization that regardless of what happened, NOTHING could wipe out what I've work for in my life because did I really work for money or financial gain anyway? Well of course I did, and it would be disingenuous of me to sit here and tell you that I wasn't financially motivated. However, I was much more motivated by the ability to help others, proving those wrong who made snarky remarks behind my back regarding how after graduating college I decided to become a full-time real estate agent and of course being the overly competitive individual I am, just the ability to crush the challenges that would lie ahead.

Here's the thing, despite what people may tell you, there's no one size fits all approach to your motivation and your inner drive. People set goals, have ambitions, and are motivated by different factors. Don't be afraid to embrace that. For me, I'll be completely honest, I was motivated simply to be the best so I could tell others to go shove it for judging me for becoming a real estate agent right out of college. Trust me, for the guys out there, meeting a girl and telling her you're a real estate agent isn't exactly going to excite her too much. Tell the girl that you're the "finance bro"? Well now, you'll be the apple of her eye. The reality? After reading this book you'll laugh at the finance bro driving a BMW working for the man and buying things he doesn't need to impress people he doesn't like. You will realize that living a life of purpose, creating value and the financial reward that comes from it will lead you to living the life you know you deserve. It will lead you to being able to create a life of happiness and pleasure for you and your family.

Money can't buy you happiness, but it can buy you time. Time that you can spend doing whatever you would like to do. Time to go on vacation, time to spend with your family, time to experience life's finest things. This book is about providing you with the road map to success as a real estate professional to buy that time. The road map I used to get to where I am today. I'm nothing special. I'm a kid from a middle-class family in Essex County. If I can do this, you can to.

Chapter 1

Making the Commitment and Setting a Schedule

Spring 2013- It's my senior year at Rutgers and I'm hungover sitting in one of my entrepreneurship classes on Livi half paying attention until I hear professor Ruff raise his voice and emphatically say, "don't fuck with my money". Okay, it's time to listen.

Ruff, a former athlete with an inner-city upbringing has brought the juice today. He's pleading to us to not fall into the societal trap of thinking that we need to, "go to school, get a job, invest in a 401k, IRA, retire then die". He is telling us how after playing college ball, like most college kids he had a couple of options. Get a 9-5 and work for the man or go into sales and bet on himself. He opted for the latter. It lead him to not only becoming a six-figure income earner within a short period of time but it allowed him to use his competitiveness, his hustle and his drive to decide how much he gets paid rather than leaving that decision up to someone else. From getting that taste of what the other side was like, he was hooked. He went on to become an NBA sports agent representing some of the league's top players as well as directing movies and of course teaching hungover college students on Wednesday's.

Is this real estate related? No. So why bring this up? When you decide to pursue something, commit to it, give it your all. Anything less is disrespectful to yourself and your family. The time you spend half-assing it will not result in anything other than frustration and time away from your loved ones.

So, what does committing to be a real estate professional mean? What does it look like? Well, at times chaotic, at other times frustrating and of course at times it will make you wish you never tried to pursue the thing. However, despite all the roadblocks, if you stay focused and persevere you will create a life by design, a life you've always dreamed of, a life of endless fulfillment. How do we get there? The first step is to make the commitment and recognize a few realities that aren't shared with people before they dive into the business.

Your broker is not going to feed you business. There is this great misconception amongst those interested in getting their real estate license that it is as simple as getting your license showing up at a brokerage and having your broker just throw you clients. This is not the case. The reality is YOU are going to be the one who is responsible for generating leads, going on appointments, showing houses, negotiating deals, paying for professional photos, doing paperwork, and following up with clients. In other words? What you just signed up for was the opportunity to run your own small business, it just happens to be under the brokerage firms name.

Gone are the days of showing up at a brokerage and sitting at a desk and just waiting for John and Jane to walk in to let you know they'd like to buy, sell or invest in real estate. There is this new thing out there called the internet which has defeated the purpose of what was once a common practice in this industry. The top agents have adjusted accordingly and are continuing to grow their businesses, the old-timers have been washed out or are now just solely relying on friends and family and some past clients to get them through the end of their careers.

These top agents account for the large majority of commissions earned in this business. In fact, the top 10% of agents make about 90% of the commissions. You might be thinking, well how the hell do I get in that top 10%? The simple answer is you treat this job like a job. Easier said than done. I can't tell you how many people get their real estate licenses and simply just have no plan. I find a lot of times it's not that they didn't want to have a plan on what they were going to do, it was a mere matter of having zero guidance of what they should do. I promise you that if you treat this like a job it will pay you more than almost any other job out there.

When you consider that on average for every $4,000,000 in homes sold you will have earned your brokerage $100,000 in commissions, that simply means that if you can sell $10,000,000 worth of real estate a year that will equate to a quarter million dollars in commissions. And no, you are not going to have to split this 50/50 with your brokerage. The first brokerage that I started with full-time had a capping commission structure which meant that from the day I joined, as soon as I made my broker $32,000 my commission split would jump from 70% to me and 30% to the broker to 100% for me.

Here are a couple of examples. If I sold $10,000,000 in homes that year, my broker would get $32,000 and I would get $218,000. What does it mean to sell $10,000,000 worth of homes? Well, if your average price point is $500,000 you would have to sell 20 homes. Therefore, you'd simply have to sell five homes every three months. Very doable. If your average price point is $250,000 it would mean 40 home sales. In other words, 10 homes every three months. Also doable, especially in that price point as those homes move super quick.

Still don't think you can do it? You can, I did. I was the first person in my family to sell real estate. My grandfather taught a real estate pre-license class hence why I got my real estate license at such a young age. Unfortunately, he never served as an active real estate agent so I couldn't really pick his brain on what to do to be a successful agent. I went into this completely and totally blind. Despite that in my first full year I sold about $4,900,000 in homes, then $8,900,000 in homes then $10,900,000 in homes and by my fourth year I was selling just around $16,000,000 in homes. This fourth year was also the time that I began to seriously invest in real estate after saving up a bunch of my earnings. That is something that we will talk about in a later chapter. For now, lets focus on setting a schedule for yourself to ensure your time is being used in the most efficient manner possible to generate more leads, close more clients and sell more homes.

I've spent time in this business as both a part-time as well as full-time real estate agent. I guess you could say on an hourly basis, most would consider me a part-timer. However, from an efficiency perspective I typically can get more done in one hour than most agents can in a week. I do not say that to toot my own horn or in a narcissistic manner but rather to show you that with the proper scheduling and systems in place you can be incredibly productive in short time blocks. Let's start with systems because once you have the proper systems in place it will allow you to then create an incredibly efficient schedule.

The first system that you should purchase when becoming a real estate agent is a power dialer. What the hell is this? A power dialer is a system where you dial into a calling center located in who knows where after creating a data set of numbers to call. When you call this calling center it will then connect you with a triple line dialer and allow your phone to dial three numbers at once and the first person who picks up is who you talk to. If two people pick up simultaneously, one of them will get a callback message which you can set to say anything. For example, my callback message is a recording of me saying, "hello… hello? I'm sorry I have bad connection let me call you right back". And the people who just straight up do not answer will get a, "drop message" which is just a pre-recorded voicemail that you make before calling this data set. As I'm writing this, I'm laughing to myself because what I just described sounds like some mad scientist shit when in reality I'm the most non-savvy tech person you'll meet and anyone can do that.

The system that I use as a power dialer is through Mojosells.com. Mojo's triple line dialer has the capability of dialing over 300 numbers per hour (if no one answers). Mojo has great customer service, so they will show you step by step how to use their systems and on top of that they even sell call lists if you want to buy lists from them. These lists include data for recent expired listings, for sale by owners and just general phone numbers through my personal favorite add-on of theirs, the neighborhood search feature. In a later chapter we will go through exactly what to say when you call these people and the primary objections you will get from them and how to overcome them. Mojo will also serve as a CRM for your business as well and allow you to schedule/track appointments and make client files to keep track of communication with individual clients. It is truly an incredible system and it starts at only $150/month and with the add-ons it should not cost you more than $200/month. And no, they do not pay me to gas them up.

For those scraping by right now or on a tight budget, you may look at that $150-$200/month number and think that is a lot of money. Change your mindset to a return on investment/return on time mindset. I was in the same position as you. I had graduated college with $55,000 in student loans, extremely limited savings and no financial support from my mother as she had her own bills and obligations to take care of (most importantly of course was making me dinner). However, I also realized that by investing in this system it would allow me to maximize my time and efforts and ultimately would pay for itself and then some. Boy oh boy did it ever pay for itself. I can honestly say that the cold calls that I made from simply investing in this system resulted in well over $1,000,000 in commissions earned, 100% of which is exclusively because I had a power dialer. Over the course of 5 years I paid about $10,000 to Mojo and in return I made well over $1,000,000 from the contacts I made on those calls. If I told you that you could invest $10,000 in something and within five years it'd turn into $1,000,000+ would you find $175/month? You sure would and you sure will because just one hour of using it a day can go a very long way.

If you are going to start in this business on a part-time basis let's just make the assumption that you are currently working a Monday-Friday 9-5 and cannot financially afford to drop your current employment to work a 100% commission based job.

Option 1: The one-hour workday. What I call the one-hour workday for those embarking on this journey part-time would consist of either going door to door or prospecting from your office or home over the phone using a power dialer from 5:30-6:30 Monday-Friday. From my experience doing this, these are the times that the most people are home, and you'll get the most contacts. Over the course of this hour you should be able to dial around 150 numbers and contact at least 20 people. Of those 20, your goal is to get one person who is looking to sell their home within the next 12 months. It might not sound like much but trust me if you are consistent with this over time, it's going to add up. It will equate to 20 people per month or 240 people per year. You're not going to land all 240 but even if you just land 10% of them, that is 24 sales and 24 sales at a $500k price point would be $12,000,000 in sales volume, which is on average $300,000 in gross commissions earned. Consistency is the key here. Be disciplined. It is just an hour a day. Later in the chapter on prospecting we'll discuss how to properly follow up with these people.

Option 2: The two-hour workday. To keep it simple you could just do option one over two hours or you could set up an alternative schedule. Extending option one over two hours would probably be best but if you want to get creative and you're the type that likes to engage people, you could push out some content and run some ads. I would suggest doing your cold calls/door to door for 60 or 90 minutes and spend the other 60 to 30 minutes respectively making videos that you post to your Facebook business page. What could these videos include? Focus on four towns and maybe make a video every day as part of a series called, "What Sold Today". In this series you simply explain to those markets what sold that day, and the details of the sale. All that information will be found in the MLS. You can also just do that once a week and run it as a, "What Sold This Week" series. Be sure to always have energy, enthusiasm, and confidence in this video along with of course starting/ending the video with your name, contact info and a call to action. We will talk about this as well in the prospecting chapter.

Now if you are going to dive in head first, burn the boats and go full-time, your schedule will obviously be different as you will have more time. In a full-time scenario I believe it is best to time block 4 hours a day of strict prospecting. In these hours do not allow anything else other than an emergency to distract you. It is okay to take hours to get back to clients. Here I am going to lay out your entire schedule for the day, even including things not related to real estate as I feel there are some little things you can do to set up your day for success.

6am: Wakeup

6:10am-7am: Exercise. This can be as simple as going for a 50 minute walk, riding a stationary bike or joining a gym and doing high intensity workouts. It is critically important in my opinion to exercise.

7am-7:30am: Eat a light breakfast. Nothing too heavy, keep it light and be cognizant of your macros. Also, be sure to drink a lot of water throughout the day. Ideally, I try to put down a gallon of water a day as this will keep your energy high and keep your mind firing on all cylinders.

7:30am-8:30am: Shower and get ready for the day.

8:30am-8:45am: Commute to your office.

8:45-9am: Set up your workstation and where you will be prospecting from.

9am-1pm: Prospect, prospect, and prospect. We will cover the different types of scripts and dialogues to use on calls in the prospecting chapters. I'd recommend going for 50 minutes at a time then taking 10-minute breaks to just walk around and get some fresh air. I usually find that keeps me the most productive. Stay off social media in those ten-minute breaks as that could really distract you and throw you off your game.

1pm-2pm: Take an hour lunch and relax. If you're working from home, you can prep your lunch the night before and eat for about 10 minutes and then lay down and even take a short little nap for 30 minutes. That is often what I would do as it would rejuvenate me for the afternoon.

2pm-3pm: Go on the MLS and see what was recently listed and if it fits any of your clients needs. Checking the MLS every day will also turn you into an expert in these markets. During this time also return all emails and phone calls that you missed earlier in the day.

3pm-4pm: Prepare for any appointments that you have in your appointment window.

4pm-6pm: Appointment window. This is when you will go on listing appointments with sellers and show buyers homes.

For now, these are some samples of schedules that you can adopt and follow. As you see above, I've mentioned numerous activities to partake in during those windows. In the following chapters we will go into detail regarding the best practices for each of those individual time blocks. How to prospect over the phone, how to follow up with clients, what to do on client appointments with buyers/sellers. So, if you feel as though that all looks great but how do I do it? Turn the page.

Chapter 2

Prospect, Prospect, Prospect

I remember being at a Rutgers football camp my junior year of high school when Greg Schiano stood before us and said, "men, get comfortable being uncomfortable". As I teenager my first thought was, what the hell is this guy saying. Then, I thought about it. Get comfortable being uncomfortable. Life isn't always easy, you will deal with adversity, you will deal with tough times but we are 100% in control of how we handle these situations. Etch this phrase into your memory and you will be wildly successful in this prospecting game that we are about to discuss.

Be thankful when someone curses you off and hangs up the phone on you in five seconds. Be thankful when someone slams a door in your face when door knocking (full disclosure I've probably knocked on 10,000+ doors and I can count on one hand how many times someone has actually slammed a door in my face. People aren't nearly as tough in person as they are on the phones).

Why am I saying this? Which would you prefer, a nice lady talks to you on the phone for 20 minutes and at the end of the call she tells you that she has no intention of ever selling and will only leave that house in a box to meet Jesus or a mean nasty lewd man curses you off in five seconds and says never call me again? Personally, I prefer the latter. Why? I have the ability through a power dialer to call up to 360 numbers an hour, therefore if someone is keeping me on for 20 minutes and we'll never do business together that is a lot of lost opportunity time where I could've kept ripping through calls and dialed upwards of 100 people in those same 20 minutes. The guy who curses me off and hangs up after five seconds will be comical to me, it'll make me have a good laugh and immediately my dialer will auto dial three more phone numbers. Emotionally, the nice old lady may make you feel better but efficiently the asshole cursing you off is so much better for you. Get comfortable being uncomfortable.

There are so many different ways to get in front of people prospecting. There is what I like to call proactive prospecting and reactive prospecting. Proactive prospecting is when you are actively reaching out to people and engaging them live whether it be over the phone or in person. Reactive prospecting is throwing ads out there and hoping people see them and reach out to you. We'll talk about both however I am a much bigger fan of proactive marketing as it is way more effective and also less expensive. More effective, less expensive? Sign me up.

Proactive Prospecting:

1. Phones

2. Door knocking

Reactive Prospecting:

1. Handwritten Follow-ups

2. Online Advertising

3. Just Sold Mailers

Let's start with prospecting over the phone and door knocking. Going back to chapter one it is essential that you first subscribe to a power dialer service like Mojosells.com. Everything that I am about to discuss is under the assumption that you have a power dialer. There are five main targets when prospecting over the phone. Those are as follows:

1. Circle Prospecting: To put it bluntly, these are just straight up cold calls. Some call this, "farming". You are essentially just mapping out neighborhoods through your power dialer and just calling every single house in those neighborhoods. The language, tonality, and verbiage you use on these calls is very important. You also must have a reason prepared for why you are calling. Are you calling because you actually have a client looking in that neighborhood or are you calling because you've noticed on your company's website or even public real estate sites that there seems to be a lot of traffic and views on homes in that neighborhood indicating that there are droves of people trying to get into that area? Keep in mind, you do not want to always play the card of, "I have a highly qualified buyer who would like to buy your home". If you do this you either

A. Better be telling the truth

B. Better hope if they agree to allow you to bring that buyer direct that your buyer will proceed and purchase

Do not put all your eggs in one basket. It is okay to let them know you have someone interested. It is also okay to be transparent and honest and let them know, you can't guarantee that they'll buy their home. This way if the buyer doesn't offer, you don't blow the chance of getting the listing. I am going to go through my script below to show you the very simple script to use.

Keep in mind that when using a power dialer, you will have the list in front of you of the three numbers currently being dialed. Let's now role play a woman picking up who's last name is Smith and lives on Main Street:

Mrs. Smith: Hello?

You: Hello, Mrs. Smith? (Tone inflection is key here)

Mrs. Smith: Yes, may I ask who is calling?

You: Hey Mrs. Smith! This is Kyle Kovats from XYZ realty, how are you? (The tone you're going to want to use here is a tone as if you are talking to someone on the phone or in person who you just saw/talked to for the first time in five years and you're excited to see/talk to them)

Option 1: Mrs. Smith: Hi, I am good. (If you were good with your tone inflection it's one of those scenario's where the person on the phone responds almost in a confused manner while thinking, "do I know this person")

Option 2 Mrs. Smith: Hi, can I help you?/ Hi, who are you? (This is if your tone inflection either wasn't great or they're just not having it)

You: Hey, I was just wondering, by any chance are you interested in selling your home on Main Street? (this will be your response regardless of whether she goes option 1 or 2. Again, your tone inflection is HUGE here. Ask this in a really questioning and inquiring type of tonality)

Option 1: Mrs. Smith: Oh no, we're not interested in moving at the moment, thanks for asking though.

Option 2: Mrs. Smith: Well why do you ask?

You: Well, the reason I ask is because we currently have a lot of buyers visiting our website looking for homes in town but as I'm sure you've seen, there's just not a whole lot hitting the market so I just wanted to see if you'd have any interest in having qualified buyers brought your way.

Option 1: Mrs. Smith: Yeah, I'm sorry were just not interested but best of luck to you.

You: Option 1 Response: I appreciate it thanks Mrs. Smith. Just one more question. By any chance do you know of any neighbors that may be interested? And trust me I promise not to tell them you told me. (Say this is a very friendly almost laughing tone at the end. If you feel they are a cordial person maybe even sneak in a 'any neighbors you'd really like to see move that you want me to call')

Option 2: Mrs. Smith: Well that's interesting. We have discussed selling but we're just not sure we're ready yet. We're not really sure what we could even get for the house.

You: Option 2 Response: I totally understand. I'm pretty much right around the corner and would be happy to swing by for a quick walk-through to give you a free estimate of value. I could even come by later this week on Friday afternoon or even over the weekend on Saturday, which would work best for your schedule? And Mrs. Smith, I wouldn't be coming over and shoving papers in your face or anything, merely just to meet and do a walk-through and if afterwards you feel the number sounds about right we can at a later time discuss perhaps working together. Fair? (try to end sentences with fair, no one ever responds with, "that's not fair")

2. Just Sold Script: This is arguably my favorite cold calling script. Why? It is the easiest one and the one that in my opinion generates the most quality leads and opens up the lines of communication. The point of the just sold script is to call homeowners within a reasonable radius of a home that just sold and let them simply know that a house just sold and share the information about it with them. The goal of this call is to hopefully find people who are intrigued by the story that you are laying out and get them to open up about being interested in potentially selling their home as well.

   Here is the beauty of this script, the house you are calling them about doesn't necessarily have to be one either you or even your firm sold. Sharing information about a home recently sold and the number it sold for is public information, making the opportunities endless to use this script. Ideally, you'd like to find homes that either sold in a very short period of time or for above asking price as these are the stories that pique homeowners interest the most and leave them wondering how much they can get for their home and if they should consider selling now.

Let's role play through a script now. Let's make the following assumptions. Mrs. Smith picks up the phone and she lives on Park Street and a house around the corner on Court Street was listed for $500,000 and just sold for $525,000 after only being on the market for six days.

Mrs. Smith: Hello?

You: Hello, Mrs. Smith? (Similar tone inflections from the prior example)

Mrs. Smith: May I ask who I'm speaking with?

You: Hey Mrs. Smith, it's Kyle Kovats from XYZ Realty, how are you?

Mrs. Smith: Good, may I help you?

You: Hey Mrs. Smith, I was just calling to see, by any chance are you interested in selling your home on Main Street?

Mrs. Smith: Why do you ask?

You: The reason I ask is we (use the word we as your friend. "We" can mean anything. It can me you, your team, your brokerage or the real estate industry) just sold a house around the corner from you on Court Street, it was a 4 bedroom and 2 bath home and we had it listed for $500,000 and after multiple bids and only six days on the market it sold for $525,000. There were a number of qualified buyers who lost out on this house so I just wanted to see if you'd have any interest in having qualified buyers brought your way.

Mrs. Smith: Wow, that's impressive. We haven't really thought much about it but what do you think we could get for our house?

You: Well, it's hard to say. Being local here and knowing the neighborhood, I'm familiar with your house from the outside (use google maps and pull up an exterior photo and describe the exterior of her house at this time. The beauty of MOJO is it has a direct link for google for that exact house when they answer the phone) but obviously I've never been inside. Can you tell me a little bit about the inside of your home?

Mrs. Smith: Sure it's a 4 bedroom, 2.5 bath center hall colonial. We have a 2-car garage, a finished basement, our bathrooms and kitchens were updated about 10 years ago and our rooms are pretty good size.

You: Impressive that all sounds great. I could always give you a general ballpark figure for your home but it won't be entirely accurate so I don't want to mislead you. I am however pretty much right around the corner as I'm local and I can swing by later this week on Friday afternoon or on Saturday earlier in the day to do a quick walk-through and put together a very accurate estimate. Which would work best for you?

Mrs. Smith: Well, I don't want to waste your time, we don't know if we're going to be selling for sure right at this very moment (This doesn't matter, still try to set an appointment because this is about relationship building and long term pipeline building)

You: Oh trust me, it wouldn't be a waste of my time and it's a relatively quick thing. Does Friday afternoon work or does Saturday morning work better?

Mrs. Smith: Let's do Friday afternoon around 3pm.

You: Great, I will see you then and if for some reason something changes with your schedule, feel free to give me a call back and we will re-arrange. Looking forward to Friday!

3. Just Listed Script: This is another relatively easy script. Here you are calling people within the general vicinity of a listing in which you or your brokerage recently just listed to see if nearby homeowners know of any potential buyers who may be interested. You are doing this for two reasons. First, do they actually know any friends or family members who may be interested. You'd be surprised how many people do actually know friends or family members who may be interested. To completely honest though, the real reason

that you are doing this is to showcase your work ethic and marketing efforts to neighbors.

I personally prefer to do this in person. I can't express to you how impressive it is to homeowners when you show up at their door marketing a nearby property. In their heads they think to themselves, wow this agent is going over and above to get this house sold, when it comes time for us to sell our house we know who to call. When going door to door, be professional, be friendly, be likeable, and smile. Make people comfortable with you. A great time to do this is the 3-4 days leading up to an open house you are hosting therefore allowing you to invite them to the open house as well.

Let's role play through a script now. Let's make the following assumptions. We are going door to door, we have zero clue what the name of the person is who answers the door and we just listed a house around the corner on Godfrey Ave.

You: Ring Door Bell

Man: Opens door

Man: Can I help you?

You: Hey, by any chance do you know anyone looking to move into this neighborhood?

Now I've done this to 10's of thousands of doors. You might be asking yourself, hold on, you don't first introduce yourself? My answer is a big fat NO. Why? Well, when I first started going door to door I'd wear a suit and bring a bag with me. The bag was filled with papers that I intended on handing out to people. Well guess what? People wouldn't even answer the door. They'd just peak out and say, "no we're not interested". For all they knew I had a brief case of money I wanted to give to them! The truth is, I looked too much like a salesman. I got everything from people from, "we're not interested", "we already know who we're voting for", "we're catholic". What? We're catholic? Well turns out I was going door to door in a neighborhood that frequently had missionaries knocking on doors and after the third time I got that response I begged the person to come to the door and I said, can I just be real for a second and ask why people keep telling me their religion in this neighborhood? They then told me that they thought I was a missionary because they were common in the neighborhood.

What do I do now? I go dressed very casual with no bag. By casual I mean something like jeans and polo or khaki shorts and a polo when it's hot out. I simply just get right into it when they answer the door. I used to try to introduce myself by saying, "Hey it's Kyle Kovats from Keller Williams Realty" and then boom, the sales wall would go up. When you get right into it you can immediately read their facial expression to see if they're interested upon asking the question. Alright, let's continue with this script.

Man: Umm, that's an odd question. Who are you and why are you asking?

You: I'm a real estate agent with XYZ Realty and I'm asking because we just listed a house around the corner on Godfrey and we're having an open house on Sunday and just wanted to see if you might know anyone who would be interested.

Man: Ahh, makes sense. Unfortunately, I don't know anyone who would be interested but if I hear of someone I'll definitely let them know. Good for you for going door to door, I appreciate the hard work. Do you have a business card?

You: Yes I do sir. Here you go. Hey, your house ain't too shabby. When are you going to be selling so I can go door to door for you? (Say this in a joking tonality, they'll usually almost always laugh along with you but sometimes even spill the beans by saying something along the lines of, "we're not too far off, keep us in mind for the next five years or so". Stay in touch with this person if that's the case and follow up with a handwritten letter thanking them for taking time to speak with you.)

4. Expired Listing Script: Expired listings are sometimes referred to as the low hanging fruit of prospecting. In other words, the easiest to convert into a listing. Expired listings are homes that were just listed with another agency for about six months and failed to sell. Almost always this is due to being overpriced. On the bright side, these people have shown already that they are on board with listing their home with an agent so really your job here is to set an

appointment and get them to price and prep their home right so you can sell it for them. In a later chapter we are going to go into detail of getting your clients to price their own house without them even knowing they just picked their list price. It's a tactic that I've used successfully for years and it's essential to ensure the house does in fact sell and not just sit on the market.

Usually with expired listings there are a number of objections these owners will pose to you. "Why are you calling me now if you have buyers. Why didn't you just bring buyers to my home when we had it on the market?". "I'm not lowering my price". "I've already been called by 30 agents". Again, in later chapters we'll dedicate an entire section on how to deal with common objections.

Let's role play through a script now. Let's make the following assumptions. You're calling the Jones family on Plymouth Street. They just had their 4 bedroom, 2.5 bath colonial on the market for 6 months originally listed at $700k and reduced down to $670k before ultimately expiring after six months on the market.

Mrs. Jones: Hello?

You: Mrs. Jones?

Mrs. Jones: Who's calling?

You: Hey Mrs. Jones, it's Kyle Kovats from XYZ Realty, how's it going today?

Mrs. Jones: I'm not interested I've had 20 of you call me today.

You: I get it Mrs. Jones, I totally hear you. I was just calling because your home popped up in my system as an expired listing and I wanted to see when you were going to be interviewing agents for the job of selling your home.

Mrs. Jones: We're taking a break, we just had it on the market for six months and it didn't sell. I don't know why all of a sudden all you agents are calling. Where were you all the past six months?

You: I hear ya Mrs. Jones. I'd be incredibly frustrated as well. (Always acknowledge what they say previously and then keep it moving) I imagine all you wanted was to just get your home on the market, sell it and move onto your next home. I actually specialize in selling homes like yours in this exact situation unlike most agents. By any chance are you familiar with the techniques I use to sell homes?

Mrs. Jones: No but I'm not really interested at this time just yet.

You: I get that, I totally do. Mrs. Jones, can I just ask you one question? Where were you planning on moving to if your home did in fact sell?

Mrs. Jones: Well we were planning on moving to Florida and now it's the fall and we're going to be stuck in cold dreary New Jersey.

You: Ahh, yes. I'd much prefer to be at or near a beach myself over a winter in Jersey (say this in a friendly laughing tonality). Let me ask you, and I mean this sincerely not just bullshitting you, (recognize the fact they believe they're being bullshitted on all these calls they keep getting. BE REAL) if I could get your home sold for you in the next couple months and get you down to Florida in rather short order would that be something you'd be interested in?

Mrs. Jones: Well, yeah of course but I'm skeptical of all you agents.

You: I hear ya, and I would be too. Trust me I deal with a lot of these agents and there are a lot of what I call Bullshitors rather than Realtors® in this business. But honestly, I do think I could probably make that happen for you. I can't say for sure and don't want to make any promises until I see your home in person and meet with you. I am selective in homes that I do in fact list because I'm not the type to waste my time and money or your time and emotion in listing a home I don't think will sell. It probably won't take more than 30-45 minutes for me to determine if I think I can get it done. By any chance would Friday afternoon work for me to swing by or would Saturday morning work better?

Mrs. Jones: I just don't know. I told my husband we'd take a break with having the home on the market for a little bit. I'd have to first ask him.

You: Understandable. If he did hypothetically say he was on board, would Friday afternoon around 4pm work?

Mrs. Jones: Yeah, that would probably work.

You: Mrs. Jones, why don't we do this. Let's pencil in 4pm on Friday and then if your husband says he has no interest, just call me back and we can cancel or reschedule, how's that?

Mrs. Jones: I guess we can do that. (Boom appointment set)

However, sometimes Mrs. Jones might say something like this,

Mrs. Jones: I don't want to feel like I'm rushing into anything. Let me first check with him before setting any tentative dates.

You: Sure, I get it Mrs. Jones. I hope that I'm not coming off pushy or anything, that's not my intent but just know that if we have a buyer come to see your home, I am always going to try to strike the iron while it's hot and convert them into offering on your home rather than letting them walk away. Kind of how I'm trying to set an appointment with you rather than just walking away like many agents often do. Does that make sense? (You just flipped the script).

5. For Sale By Owner Script: Another script that falls on the low hanging fruit tree is the for sale by owner script often called the FSBO (pronounced fizz-bo). These are owners who are clearly interested in selling their home but they're trying to do so on their own to avoid paying commission.

The whole key to this script is to convince them that after listing with you and even paying commission that they'll net more money in their pocket if they had otherwise done it all by themselves. The beauty of this is, it's the truth. The national stats have shown that on average homes listed with agents sell for about 17% more than those list with for sale by owners. Why is that? Well, over 90% of buyers are represented by real estate agents, so do you think it's smart to knock 90% of your buyer pool out before you even start? The other good news here is the stats show that the large majority of FSBO's eventually wind up listing with an agent, it's just a matter of time.

Let's role play through a script now. Let's make the following assumptions. You're calling the Walsh's and they currently have their home on Gordon Road listed FSBO.

Mr. Walsh: Hello?

You: Hello, Mr. Walsh?

Mr. Walsh: Yes, may I ask who I'm speaking with?

You: Hey Mr. Walsh, it's Kyle Kovats from XYZ Realty how's it going today.

Mr. Walsh: I'm good. We're selling for sale by owner we're not interested in listing with an agent, I don't want to waste your time.

You: Sure, thank you. I appreciate you being so straight forward. Can I just ask one question? Why did you decided to sell for sale by owner rather than with a professional agent like myself?

Mr. Walsh: To save commission obviously. I don't want to pay 5% of my sales price to a real estate agent.

You: That's what I figured. So how much you net in your pocket after selling is obviously important to you.

Mr. Walsh: Well of course, I mean who wouldn't that be important to?

You: You're right probably a dumb thing for me to say Mr. Walsh. Mr. Walsh, I've sold a lot of homes that were originally listed as for sale by owners like yours. If I could show you an approach to getting your home sold that will net you more money in your pocket even after paying commission than you would have otherwise gotten selling for sale by owner would you be willing to have a short sit down with me to discuss?

Mr. Walsh: Not really, I think I'll be able to get this done and make more money myself.

You: I get that and that very well may be the case, you sound like a sharp guy. To be completely honest, I've never been in your house and I can't say for sure at this very moment whether or not I'm 100% confident in my ability to get you more money. Frankly, sometimes it is the case that you're better off dealing with it on your own. However, I would love the opportunity to meet with you to do a walk-through and discuss the different things I will do to net you more money if I feel I can. Worst case scenario is maybe you pick up a few ideas from me that you can use yourself. Best case scenario is I take all the work off your plate and net you more money in your pocket at the end of transaction. Mr. Walsh, would you be willing to invest just maybe 30-45 minutes of your time to meet with me further discuss?

Mr. Walsh: You know what, I appreciate that you're being straight with me as well. I'm not opposed to at least hearing what you have to say.

You: Would Friday afternoon work or does Saturday morning work better for you?

Congrats, you've set the appointment. The whole key here is, DO NOT tell them they can't sell on their own. In fact, embrace the fact they can sell on their own, just pivot to framing it as they will net less money. Most agents make the mistake of saying, "you can't sell it by yourself!" That's bullshit. Anyone can sell by themselves. How much they can sell for is the real question.

Let's pivot now to reactive marketing. Reactive marketing does work however it could be costly and is not nearly as effective as proactive marketing. I'm going to share with you the most effective forms of reactive marketing that I have personally implemented as well as some other forms that I have not personally implemented but have discussed with other agents.

1. The Follow-Up Handwritten Letter: Remember how we just discussed actively prospecting? Well, when you are circle prospecting, just listed, just sold, you often are going to

find people who aren't ready just yet. They may be ready in 1, 2, 3 years' time though and it is important to stay in front of these people and what we call, "nurture" the relationship.

Right after you get off the phone with them or after you've door knocked them and they've told you they are considering selling but not for another 1, 2, 3 years, immediately hand write a letter thanking them for taking the time to speak with you. Be sure to end the letter with, "when the time comes that you do decide you're ready to have qualified buyers brought your way, just give me a buzz. I'm right around the corner and would be honored to help."

These little things really do go a long way. It's so easy to put someone onto what we call a "drip campaign" and have automatic generic emails or letters sent their way. That is tacky and it makes them feel like just one of hundreds. When you send a personalized handwritten letter, while yes, it will take more time to put together, it will also pack a much bigger punch and have a significantly stronger impact.

This is not to say I don't send generic mail pieces out to these people, I do. However, they are custom and handwritten. Here is what I do. After I have them in my CRM system, I create files for them. For example, files for all of my prospective sellers in North Caldwell. I will then craft a custom letter to all my leads in North Caldwell. I will handwrite it in BLUE ink and then make color copies of it and send it to them and handwrite their name and address on the envelope. The reason I am being sure to emphasize the blue ink part is because when you make photocopies of black ink, it is very obvious it is copied. When you photocopy blue ink it comes out looking like it's still actually freshly handwritten.

These update letters should give them a direct update on their town's real estate market. Include in here stats such as recently sold homes, days on market, sales to list price ratio, and then a tip at the end for them to keep in mind. These types of informative letters are letters that they will actually read. Keep it short, sweet, and direct.

2. Facebook Ads: I find these to be extremely cost effective and very easy to zone in on potential clients. I will preface this by saying that Facebook is constantly changing their rules and regulations for advertising so by the time you read this, the rules could have changed.

You can use Facebook ads for a number of different things such as marketing a listing that you have, marketing an open house that you have coming up or even just creating a platform for yourself as a local real estate expert by doing short videos on market updates. These three avenues are the ones that I most frequently utilize. The first step is obviously to make a Facebook business page. That's simple enough to figure out on your own, I'm not going to get into a how-to on that.

Let's start with marketing an upcoming open house that you have. In your ad you're going to want to make it no more then four sentences and have about six pictures in the ad.

I would recommend selecting the option in the ad to add a "message" button which is essentially a call to action for people to just click "message" to message you direct on your Facebook page with questions. I would also suggest not putting the list price in the ad as this will inevitably lead to more people commenting and messaging asking for info which will allow you to converse with them via messenger and possibly try to convert them to clients. Here is a sample of an ad that I recently ran and led to some solid traffic at an open house.

"ROSELAND: Open House at 95 Eagle Rock Ave on Sunday from 12-2pm. Immaculate 4 bedroom 2.5 bath home located just steps away from NYC public transportation. Perennial top school district in NJ and ranked by niche.com as the #4 school district for high school athletes in NJ out of over 600 schools! The town and the home offer it all! See you on Sunday!"

As you'll notice in this ad, I talked very little about the actual house. Why is that? Well the six pictures should be able to showcase the most positive features of the house so therefore our ad focuses on things that not the average person would know about the house/location/town.

In this ad I opted to pinpoint a location and target the 10 mile radius around this home as well as the Hoboken, Jersey City and Weehawken markets searching for prospective buyers who may be interested in moving just about 25 minutes away to the suburbs. I set my budget for $25/day for 6 days leading up to the open house. Why $25/day? I went to a NAR 30 under 30 conference one year and they had a master marketer explain that the $25/day threshold is what really jumps you to the top and allows you to get in front of the most people. Science, I guess?

Next, we focus on marketing a listing that you have. If I am not running an ad to push traffic to an open house, then I focus on just generally marketing a listing that I have and trying to start conversations via Facebook messenger with interested parties. It is essential that you select the add message button when running these ads as it will allow an interested individual to instantly message you the moment they see the ad.

Keep in mind, 99% of the time the person who messages you is not going to buy that very home. While you are placing the ad in hopes of selling that home, to be truthful the reason we place it is to find buyers who aren't working with agents and trying to convert them into our clients. The beauty of Facebook is that when these people message you, you will have their names and where they are from by looking at their profile. This will allow you to follow up with a handwritten note and ultimately get an idea for what type of house they might be looking to sell.

When they do in fact message you, the first goal is to see if you could actually sell them the home they messaged you about. However, from my experience, a lot of the time they are just in the really early stages of their search and are nosey as to what the price is and getting more information about the listing. If you feel the house isn't for them, open up into a dialog and ask two simple questions. First, how long have they been looking for homes. Second, who are they currently working with as an agent. The second question will tell you if it's worth spending more time talking with them. If they say, "we're working with my cousin John Smith from XYZ Realty", then you are not going to convert them. If they say, "we're really early in our search and don't have an agent yet", then you are going to try to set some kind of phone call or in person meeting with them. Your next message should be asking them, when they plan on interviewing the right agent for the job of representing them in their home search along with a sentence or two about some unique things you do for buyers and how of course it's all a free service as the seller pays commission. It always helps to have a quick little five-minute video on deck of you discussing your services as a buyer's agent.

Try to convert these people as quickly as possible. If you let them sit for too long, they'll lose interest and move on. Try to schedule the appointment to meet or speak with them over the phone ASAP. Zoom meetings are preferred over speaking on the phone as well. Face to face interaction goes a long way.

The last type of general Facebook ads would be just creating a general platform for yourself. Just simply doing a monthly market update that you run for about a week and drop $25/day into will get you right in front of the people you want to target all while providing valuable information while they're not left feeling like they're being sold.

What exactly would this monthly market update look like? Let's say you were doing an October market recap. You're going to run this video the first week of November. In preparation for this video you're going to want to pull all of the stats off the MLS for that particular town. The key metrics to focus on are days on market, sales to list price ratio, and how many new listings hit the market. We want to try to keep this video to three to five minutes to ensure it is watched and keeps the audience engaged.

Always end the video with some type of call to action. For example, my common call to action is, "if you would like to learn more about local market stats or would like a free estimate of value of what a buyer would be willing to pay for your home in todays market, please message me and we'll set up a call to discuss further".

These do not always turn into immediate business, so you must be consistent. I cannot tell you how many times I've gotten calls out of the blue of someone saying they're interested in selling their home and they'd like to have me over to discuss because they've seen my videos on Facebook and they want a strong local agent like myself.

3. Mailers: This is the least effective reactive marketing from my experience. I only send out one type of mailer and that is the, "just sold" mailer. If I just sold a home in a neighborhood, once in a while I'll send this out if I feel the sale

provided some kind of eye popping number whether it be a really high price, significantly above asking, or sold in just a few days. The response rate on mailers is statistically only between 1%-2% so keep in mind that you shouldn't expect all that much from these.

In my opinion it is far more effective and obviously free to just call the entire neighborhood or go door to door using the just sold script. Personally, I wouldn't waste your money on mailers, but the choice is yours.

The moral of this chapter? PROSPECT, PROSPECT, PROSPECT. Prospecting is the number one revenue generating activity that you can partake in. It is the lifeblood of your business. You must constantly be staying in front of people. If you can consistently prospect you will consistently be a top producing agent

Chapter 3

Dealing With Buyers

This might sound obvious but without buyers there are no sales. When you first start off in the real estate business, buyers are going to be the easiest clients to obtain. Sellers are often looking for experienced agents who have sold homes as they are likely going to pay out five-figures in commissions. However, buyers often feel neglected considering the top agents don't always pay much mind to them because that would involve the top agent running around on nights and weekends showing homes for what could take months and they just don't have the patience anymore to do that.

For starters, what are the main avenues of acquiring buyer clients? The top three in order are open houses, friends and family, referral from top agents in your brokerage.

1. Open Houses: The reality of open houses is that only 2% of open houses lead to a consummated sale. So, the question then becomes, why would agents even waste their time having open houses? The simple answer is because it is the

number one avenue for meeting buyers. We talked in the prospecting chapter about going through the, "just listed" script and door knocking for an upcoming open house. Now let's talk about hosting that open house and effective ways in which you can convert these unrepresented buyers into clients and ultimately close more sales.

First and foremost, when hosting the open house look professional. Dress nice, smell good, and have energy, enthusiasm, and confidence. When a couple rings the doorbell or opens the door to the open house greet them, shake their hands and introduce yourself. Then, the first question that you want to ask them is the following. "John and Jane great to meet you, are you going to meeting your agent here today or are you alone?". The reason for this question is to simply find out if they already have an agent they are working with or if they are prospects you should spend time with. If they tell you they are already working with an agent from ABC Realty then give them the layout of the house and tell them to feel free to walk-through at their own pace and if they have any questions to let you know. If they tell you something along the lines of, "we are kind of early in our search and don't have an agent yet, is that okay?". Then, give them a personal tour through the house and begin a conversation to build rapport.

When giving them the tour throughout the home you're going to want to bring up some very specific topics which will allow you to steer the conversation down the path that leads to you setting a meeting with them to make them exclusive buyers agency clients of yours. The first leading question I ask after we've been together for a few minutes and I feel like we're connecting is, "so how long have you guys been looking for?". Usually if they don't have an agent yet their answer will include something indicating that they just kind of started looking. However, sometimes you just have buyers who truly believe that they should only be working directly with listing agents as they feel listing agents will be able to get them the best possible deal on the home. Let's run through these two scenarios and how you can respond.

A. **You:** So, how long have you guys been searching for a home?

> **Buyers:** Well, we just kind of began our search pretty recently.

> **You:** Ahh, I see. I'm sure you've noticed that not a ton of homes have been hitting the market recently, I hear a lot of buyers complaints and frustration with this which has lead me to go door to door for my clients in the neighborhoods they like to try to find homes not on the market that fit their criteria. (This almost always intrigues buyers and they follow up with the following below)

> **Buyers:** What do you mean go door to door for homes not on the market?

You: Well, when I first start working with clients we kind of sit down for about 30 minutes and go through everything they want in a home from style, finishes, neighborhood to school district. After knowing exactly what they're looking for it then allows me to search for both homes publicly on the market and also those that aren't listed by going door to door in neighborhoods they want to be in. This way we don't just have their search confined to what everyone else knows about. Ideally, I'd love to find them a home off the market so they can bid against themselves and don't have to get involved in any sort of bidding war.

Buyers: Wow, we never heard of that before.

You: Yeah, it is definitely a lot of additional work and time but at the end of the day, it is what is best for the client. I can certainly do the same for you but obviously I'd have to know your exact search criteria and considering I'm hosting an open house right now I can't just sit down for 30 minutes to go through all that with you. What are you guys doing after 2pm? (or whatever time the open house ends) We can meet up for a half hour or so to go through your criteria and then I can expand your search to off-market properties.

Buyers answer 1: Sure, we can meet. Where would you like to meet?

Buyers answer 2: We have some running around to do after this so today might not work.

You to answer 1: (If close to your office) let's meet at my office it's about 10 minutes from here. Let me take down your number right now so I can text you the address that we'll meet at.

You to answer 2: Would later in the day work or sometime during the week after work be better? We can meet at my office, at a restaurant closest to you or meet over zoom, which is best?

After this you have secured the appointment for the buyer consultation. Later in this chapter we will outline what is involved in the buyer consultation and what key points you should hit during that meeting.

B. "We are only working with listing agents" Buyer: We are only working with listing agents at this time. We are not looking for an agent to show us homes, sorry.

> **You:** I hear ya. If you don't mind me asking, is there any reason why you're only working with listing agents and adverse to seeking buyers agent representation?

> **Buyer:** Well, obviously the listing agent can get you the best deal for the house because they know exactly what the seller will accept.

> **You:** I figured that was the thought. You're not alone it's a very common misconception but the reality is, listing agents legally are not allowed to even help you negotiate price when operating as a dual agent which means to represent both buyer and seller. So even if the

agent is not me, a buyer should always look to work with a buyer's agent as a buyer's agent exclusively represents the buyer's interest and can go to bat for them in terms of negotiating price, inspection items and of course still being able to show you any house that comes on the market whether it be listed with their own firm or another firm.

Buyer: Is that really true?

You: It really is. The document that you have to sign when you begin working with any agent whether it be a listing agent or buyer's agent is called a consumer information statement and it's in that document where everything I just explained to you is laid out in writing. I'll be honest with you, who knows if we'd even be a fit to work together but you seem like great people. This open house ends around 2pm, let's meet at my office nearby at 2:15 and sit down for about 30 minutes or so to figure out exactly what you're looking for so I can then search for homes both on and off the market for you. How does that sound?

2. Friends and Family: Your friends and family are always reliable referral sources and also themselves sources for business. The key here is to avoid being what I like to call a, "secret agent". A secret agent is someone who gets their real estate license and for some odd reason doesn't tell everybody and their mothers that they now have their real estate license. A big reason for this in my opinion is the fear

of failure. The fear of telling people you got your license only to do nothing with it and feel like a failure. Failure is good. Failure is a part of life. The more times you fail the more times you succeed. So, tell everybody you know, that you have your real estate license and you're taking this thing seriously.

The best way to do this is regardless of your personality, have a serious conversation with friends about this. Even the biggest of jokers out there, if you can muster up the courage to get serious for just a moment, it will have a big long-term impact on your business. Just simply have an honest conversation with friends and family members explaining that you just got your real estate license and you really want to take this thing seriously. Make it known that if they ever need advice on real estate or are looking to buy or sell or know somebody looking to buy or sell to please reach out to you and that it'd really mean a lot.

It would also help to have a simple elevator pitch prepared for what you are going to do for buyers. It can look something like the following:

Buyers: John, I just got my real estate license and I'm really going to take this thing seriously. I feel as though there are way too many lazy complacent agents just going through the motions. So, with all the buyers that I work with, I am going to not only show them homes on the market but also work my ass off and go door to door for them knocking on doors trying to find homes off the market that aren't publicly available as well. If you, a family member or anyone you know is looking for a home, it'd really mean the world to me if you could put me in touch with them so I can help them. I promise I won't let you or them down.

That right there is powerful, quick, and effective. You simply explain what you're going to do, and you end it with a call to action along with a genuine and heartfelt compassionate plea. This will go a long way in them keeping you top of mind.

3. Referral from top agents: Most top agents don't like working directly with buyers and showing houses. The reason is buyers are time consuming. They want to see houses on nights and weekends and sometimes take months upon months before offering on something. Top agents feel they've already cut their teeth enough to not have to deal with this stuff anymore and will either actively try to avoid working with buyers or be very happy to refer buyers to other agents for referral fees. Lets go over how to approach a conversation with a top agent at your brokerage on partnering with them to service their buyers.

> **You:** Hey John, I know you're one of the top agents at the firm and just wanted to introduce myself to you. My name is Kyle Kovats, I just joined the firm and am eager to get going.

> **John:** Very nice to meet you.

You: I don't want to take up too much of your time but figured I'd just throw this out there. By any chance do you ever have buyers that you don't have enough time to service? I only ask because if that is the case I'd really be happy to work with them for a referral fee and I promise to provide true top notch service all the way down to door knocking for them in neighborhoods they are interested in.

John: I really appreciate the offer, why don't we set up a time to discuss this further. We definitely may be able to work something out here.

This conversation is usually quick and to the point. Your whole goal here is to quick elevator pitch the top agent and try to set up a meeting with them. A standard referral split for an agent giving you buyers to work with is 50/50. In other words, you two split the commission earned on the sale after the brokerage has taken their cut.

Another avenue to explore is to join a top producing real estate team at your brokerage. This is a concept gaining a whole lot of steam in the business right now. A top producing agent will form a team in order to do more business and leverage the time of others in exchange for compensation.

If you're interested in this when you first join the firm ask the broker or manager who the top agents/top teams are at the firm. Once you get their names, shoot them emails or knock on their office door to try to schedule a meeting with them. The leaders of these teams are always eager to interview hungry and talented individuals to join their team. When joining this team as a buyer's agent, the team leader will assign you buyers to work with and provide direct one on one training on how to properly service the buyer. It is a great way to start in the business as you're getting clients (albeit at lower commission splits) and you're getting direct one on one training from a top producing agent. Can't beat that!

Creating The Dream Team

After you have buyers to work with the next step is to ensure you are properly servicing them and that all starts with setting up a team for them. What I mean here is making sure this process of buying a home is as smooth, simple, and easy for them as it possibly can be. Remember we're not churning them and burning them, we are trying to create a business with a 10-20 year plan rather than a 10-20 minute plan. To do that, you must create great experiences for everyone who deals with you. This begins with creating a "team" for your clients.

When you sit down with prospective buyer clients for the buyer consultation there are a series of questions that you will go through with them which we'll get into later in this chapter but almost equally as important is to stress to them the importance of having a good team representing them at every turn.

There is a lot more to a real estate transaction than just simply finding a house, putting in an offer and having it accepted. After the offer is accepted in some states like New Jersey, you will go into an attorney review period. Afterwards, you will go into the home inspection period. And of course before all this begins, the client will first need to make sure they're approved to buy in the price point they're looking at so they'll begin by talking with a reputable mortgage broker/banker.

Mortgage Brokers/Bankers are an extremely critical piece to the transaction. You want a lender who can get your client financing but also be able to shoot them straight and just be blunt about what they can afford and what they can't afford. There will be a lot of prospective buyers out there who have played around with mortgage calculators online and believe that they can afford a $500,000 house based on the numbers they've seen on what those monthly mortgage payments will be. However, a lender may come back to them with some harsh news that with the amount of down payment they can afford, they can only get approved up to $400,000. This could be due to numerous factors whether it be credit score, loan to value ratio, debt to income ratio, etc. Rather than waste the time of both your client and yourself, finding this out right from the jump will make for a more efficient and easier transaction. Trust me, nothing is worse than having a client who is not pre-approved find out after looking for two months and finally finding their dream home that they cannot afford it. Get this taken care of up front.

So, what separates a good lender from a bad lender? From my experience, what I have found is that pretty much all lenders claim they have some kind of magical loan program that no other lender has.

I've never found this to really be the case. They all more or less offer similar loan products at relatively similar rates. The key here is finding a lender who is a top tier communicator and stays on top of things and makes sure the loan is set to close on time. Communication is by far number one here.

Throughout the transaction issues may pop up. The lender may require some additional documents, disclosures, signatures, and other items for the loan to close on time. It is imperative that they communicate this to the borrower as soon as possible to ensure that these things are getting taken care of and we're not having to delay the closing. Remember, your client very well could be selling their house and simultaneously buying this next one. Your client also could be currently renting and has given move-out notice to the landlord. Do you want to feel responsible that the lender you recommended them delayed their closing which in turn made them delay the sale of their current house or worse, left them homeless for a week if they are a renter who gave a move out notice and now have to pay storage fees for their furniture for a week? Refer good communicators. That is key.

Real Estate Attorneys can be worth their weight in gold and really alleviate much of the burden from you after offer and acceptance. In New Jersey where I operate out of, it is very common for both the buyer and seller in a transaction to hire attorneys to represent them in the sale of the property. I recognize that this may not be as common in other states. So, if you're in a state where using real estate attorneys in transactions is not common, skip over this section.

Much like the lender section, the number one thing you want in a real estate attorney is excellent communication skills. This real estate attorney (and I stress REAL ESTATE attorney) should be well versed with the real estate side of law, understand the jargon and primarily practice real estate. In a state like NJ where we have a mandatory attorney review period, the deal is not legally binding until you exit attorney review. The goal is to exit attorney review as soon as humanly possible! Therefore, if you're a buyer, you don't have to worry about a higher offer coming in. If you're a seller, you don't have to worry about a buyer changing their mind and finding something else.

The real estate attorney will also take care of the negotiations of any inspection issues that may arise, appraisal issues in the case the appraisal comes out lower than the sales price, and of course prepping the closing documents and arranging with the title company and lender the date and time which the closing will take place. If you don't know a good real estate attorney just simply ask your broker or one of the top agents in the firm who they'd recommend as a great real estate attorney.

All **Home Inspectors** are NOT created equally. While the home inspectors your clients use will all be licensed and to a similar degree know what they are looking for, they certainly will differ tremendously in, you guessed it, communication. Even more so than the lender and attorney, communication is of the utmost importance with inspectors.

Unfortunately, there are some home inspectors who are known, "alarmists". What this means is they essentially try to freak out buyers to encourage them not to buy a house. You might be wondering what they'd gain out of that. Well, this buyer is going to buy a house whether it be this one they are doing an inspection on or another house. If an inspector causes a buyer not to buy a house, a buyer will likely believe that the inspector did them a great service in causing them not to buy a, "lemon" of a house. Therefore, this results in the buyers hiring the same inspector again for their next home inspection on a different house. The inspector now gets paid for two home inspections rather than one. How common is this? A lot more common than you'd think.

You want a home inspector who is a normal human and not inspector gadget. Let me be clear, we want a home inspector that will find everything and anything possibly wrong with the home but we also want them to be able to explain it without having their eye balls burn a hole through our clients faces while they explain things without blinking for two minutes straight. Do I sound frustrated? Yes, I am. Years later I cannot stop thinking about August 2016 when I had the same home inspector kill three deals in a row when he did home inspections for buyers on homes in which I represented the seller. It was so bad, that since that day when representing sellers, I almost always ask buyers when they submit their offer who they will be using as a home inspector. If it is a certain inspector, I tell them they have to use someone else or we can't seriously consider their offer.

Here's an example of a good home inspector vs and alarmist home inspector. Let's say for example around the kitchen sink the outlets are not GFCI outlets. Construction code calls for GFCI outlets to be around water sources like sinks. The good home inspector will say, "Mr. and Mrs. Buyer, you really should have GFCI outlets around the sink. I'm going to recommend replacing these two outlets around the sink and an electrician will probably charge you $100 an outlet. It's a quick simple job." The alarmist will say, "Mr. and Mrs. Buyer, you need to replace the electric in the kitchen." See what a difference that is? Now imagine it's a first-time home buyer and they hear they need to replace the electric in the kitchen. The alarmist can cause months and months of hard work to vanish in an hour or two. You owe it to yourself and to your clients to refer good, competent, home inspectors to them.

The best way to ensure that your clients are using the, "team" we've assembled for them is to set expectations up front and lay out scenarios for them. Explain to them what to expect at each phase of the transaction. Best case, worst case, most likely. This way when different issues pop up, they don't feel caught off guard, they don't feel blindsided, they instead feel as though they were ready for this!

Laying Out the Scenarios: Best Case, Worst Case, Most Likely

Each phase of the transaction has various issues that can arise and can turn the transaction upside down. Most of the time, these issues can be easily resolved. Other times not so much. As always, we want to control what we can control and in this case that is setting expectations and laying out the scenarios and challenges that a client may be faced with.

The best case is very straight forward and does not require much in-depth explanation. In the best-case scenario you find a home, you make an offer that doesn't involve a bidding war, your offer gets accepted, attorney review is smooth, home inspection has no issues, the appraisal from the bank comes back fine and then you simply close.

Much more likely is a transaction that has variations of one or more of the following challenges listed below. It's important to have these conversations right on the onset of your working relationship with clients because once again, there is no worse scenario than them feeling blindsided.

Challenge #1, The Bidding War: Bidding wars do happen and like all real estate transactions there are two sides of the coin here. One side representing the buyer. The other side representing the seller. Since this chapter is dedicated to dealing with buyers, we will discuss how to both prep buyers for a bidding war as well as how to put them in the best possible position to succeed in becoming that winning bid. It is not always the highest offer but rather the best offer that wins!

Right at the very onset of your working relationship with a buyer, when you first sit down for a "buyer consultation", you should bring up to them the potential of being involved in a bidding war and what that looks like. Typically in most bidding wars a listing agent will have five days or so worth of showings and report back to all agents who expressed that their clients would like to submit an offer that they have X amount of offers at the moment and that final and best bids are due by 5pm on Friday (it could be any day, I'm just using Friday as the example).

A good listing agent will usually be proactive and forthcoming regarding exactly what their client is looking for that could have your offer stand out whether it be price, terms, closing date, etc. If they are not forthcoming about that then simply asking them. "Hey John, we are definitely going to be submitting an offer. What in particular is your client looking for that would have our offer standout besides price obviously."

Here are the top three items (besides price) in order of what will have your clients offer not only stand out but perhaps be accepted despite the fact that they may not even be the highest offer.

1. Language about the appraisal: One of the concerns sellers have in a bidding war is that they will sell their home for too much money. Weird concern, right? Well, here's why it's a big concern. For example, if a home was listed at $500,000 and a bidding war breaks out and your client is on board with offering $540,000 to lock this one up. That is great but the seller might be thinking, "well what if my home appraises by the bank at $510,000? Can't they just ask me to lower my price to $510,000?". The answer is yes.

   In an appraisal shortfall, the buyer reserves the right to ask the seller to lower their price to $510,000. The seller also reserves the right to deny that request and ask the buyer to make up that $30,000 in additional cash down payment to stick with their original offer of $540,000. Maybe you meet somewhere in the middle where the buyer puts down an extra $15,000 in down payment while the seller lowers their price to $525,000.

   One of the ways to alleviate this concern and really have your offer stand out is to proactively in your offer explain up front to the seller what you will do in this situation.

Rarely, if ever, will a buyer completely waive their appraisal contingency because if they bid $550,000 and an appraisal comes out at hypothetically $450,000, they have essentially agreed to increase their down payment by $100,000. They either do not have six-figures laying around or simply don't want to do it. So, instead the best practice here is to put language in the offer that says something along the lines of, "In the case of an appraisal short fall, buyer will make up the difference between the appraisal value and sales price up to a max amount of either the proposed purchase price or $10,000 above appraised amount, whichever is lower." For example, if you bid $550,000 and the appraisal comes out at $530,000, you will not ask them to lower all the way to $530,000 but rather just $540,000 in this situation.

By putting this language in an offer, you greatly increase the chances of your client not only getting the home but likely even lower than the highest offer that doesn't have similar language. Here's the thing, if someone offers $560,000 and refuses to put any language in their offer about the appraisal, it is effectively the same thing as telling the seller that if the appraisal comes out at $530,000, I'm going to ask you to lower to $530,000. Whereas with your offer that we presented above, while you are initially $10,000 lower than their offer, you would ultimately wind up $10,000 higher and be a safer bet for the seller. Again, the point of this is to ease any concerns a seller may have. By simply putting this language in the offer at the very least it makes them think why didn't others do the same?

2. Language about the home inspection: The common tie between the concerns the seller has regarding the appraisal and the home inspection is that both can lead to the seller losing money and that is something that all people want to avoid in what ultimately is a financial transaction. When you sit down with the buyer for the consultation you should be setting the expectations of what the inspection will entail, what are typical items that pop up and what is reasonable to ask versus what is unreasonable to ask. If you have done that properly, explaining the language of crafting an offer that eases the sellers concerns of what could pop up in a home inspection becomes far less complex.

I cannot express to you enough how much sellers worry about home inspections. Despite the fact that they have personally lived in this home for the past 10, 20, 30 years, they all recognize that a home inspector when combing through the house is bound to find a number of things that are wrong. The seller is fearful of a couple things. First, they just negotiated and accepted an offer at a number that they like or perhaps was even a little lower than they would've liked to have gone and now the buyer is being presented with another opportunity to whack the price down even lower. It's a proposition that I've seen cause numerous deals to fall through and not always because it was the financially smart thing to do but rather ego and feeling like they're being taken advantage of. Second, is the buyer just going to nitpick them on little trivial things and make them do 20 repairs to their home before they sell, a situation they want to avoid at all costs.

We are going to present our offer and bury all these concerns and express to the seller that they can proceed with us without having to worry about the aforementioned situations occurring. This sometimes I have found is even more important than the appraisal language we talked about previously. The home inspection is a lot more personal. The home inspection is something where you are in essence telling them that they did not take care of their home and therefore they now must pay the price. This may sound a little ridiculous but that is the way a seller views it. Whereas if the bank appraisal comes out low, it's not your fault and it's not an indictment against what they've poured their lives into over the past number of years in the place they call home.

The way in which you craft this language is important from a couple perspectives. First and foremost, protecting your client in the situation that there are some really major items that need to be addressed. Secondarily, making the seller feel comfortable going with your offer while not having to worry about being nitpicked in an inspection. Here is how I typically present this in the offer. "Buyer will not seek inspection items totaling less than $2,500 for a single item outside of code violations, structural concerns, environmental hazard, termites, mold and major mechanicals." This language here is a win-win situation for both parties. The buyer is still covered if any expensive repairs pop up or any of the other six items mentioned, while the seller is given the peace of mind that as long as the major big-ticket items are okay which they usually believe are, then they have nothing to worry about. This type of language very well could result in your client being named the winning bid despite not having the highest offer. Remember, I can't express this enough, it's not the highest bid that wins, it is the best bid that wins.

3. Language about the closing date: This one is simple and to be honest it's very rare that this would be a deal breaker or have your client's offer stand out from the competition. A standard closing date is 45-60 days after offer and acceptance. However, sometimes a client is really eager to move and they have another home that they have lined up and are ready to purchase and perhaps may want to close in 30 days. Other times, maybe the seller listed in March not knowing how long it would take to sell their home in New Jersey and move to Florida. If the sellers have school-aged kids they may not want to close for 90 days if they receive an offer in the first week because they want their kids to finish the school year.

This is not always essential language in the offer because usually you will just call the listing agent and ask them, "when does your client want to close". They will simply just tell you and usually you'll just get on board with that in your offer. There are times when you'll deal with an unprofessional agent or an agent that is a horrible communicator so therefore in a bidding war type of situation to ensure the seller knows your buyer can close on their timeframe just put simple language in the contract such as, "buyer will let seller pick closing date any time between 40-90 days after offer and acceptance". This is like saying if you were to make an offer on June 1st that you'd be okay with closing any time between around July 10th and September 1st. This will rarely be a deal breaker but it's just another item that you can put in your offer that could help your cause.

Challenge #2, The Swoop in During Attorney Review: If you're not a New Jersey agent please skip ahead as New Jersey is the only state that has a mandatory attorney review period.

As soon as you have offer and acceptance in New Jersey, you will immediately enter the attorney review period at which time the buyer and seller will hire attorneys to review the contract and make sure that all I's are dotted, t's are crossed and nothing is whacky. This may sound like a mere formality, and it should be as long as you make sure your client uses a REAL ESTATE attorney. If they don't use a real estate attorney, the attorney review can drag on and put the deal in danger of falling through because while you remain in attorney review, the buyer or seller is allowed to cancel with zero liability. It is in both parties best interests to exit attorney review and make the deal binding as quickly as possible.

As the buyer, your fear here is that if attorney review drags on that a better offer comes in and the seller cancels yours and goes with the better offer. As a professional listing agent, the proper way they should approach that scenario would be to call up the buyers agent and let them know that a stronger offer came in and before they decide to proceed with that offer, they would like to give you a second chance to improve your offer. With that said, there is no legal requirement for them to do so.

What happens if this situation does arise? As a buyers agent, you should thank the sellers agent for letting you know and just ask a simple question, "What do we have to do to improve our offer to keep this house?" They will usually give you some insight at which time you should follow up with a little test to see exactly how good that other offer is. Not that this happens often but I have been involved in these situations. That test would be along the lines of, "Thanks again for letting me know. I am going to discuss with my client and see what they'd like to do. I assume they're going to want to proceed but just want to confirm with them. You know how it goes sometimes a buyer feels like they're getting played." What the seller's agent says next is very telling. If they come back with a simple, "Okay just let me know either way", then you know they have a very strong offer. However, if they come back with, "I wouldn't tell your client to panic, I think if they just come up a little bit that the seller would be happy to stick with them", in that case you know the other offer is just barely above yours, if even at all.

Express to your client, they're not obligated to improve their offer but at the same time, the seller is not obligated to stick with them. Don't ever put them in a situation where it feels like you are forcing them to do something. Our role in this business is to simply present the facts and data to our client and provide them with the autonomy to make a decision that they feel is best.

Challenge #3, The Disastrous Home Inspection: If you have deals fall through, the home inspection will be the most likely reason. The home inspection is a critical part of the transaction as it is where any hidden or undiscovered defects to the home will be found. However, as discussed previously, not all home inspectors are created equally. It's worth repeating, make sure you refer home inspectors to your clients who know how to explain issues that they have found in the home. If you don't do this you are going to find a much larger percentage of your deals falling through and not making it to closing.

At the very first buyer consultation you should be explaining to your client some common things that pop-up in home inspections that on the surface sound like a big deal but really are not. Things such as termites, mold, regrading and having to replace electrical outlets sound like big issues, especially to first time home buyers. Reality though is that these issues are very minor and easily corrected.

As long as the termites have not caused structural damage to a home then all the seller will do is order a pest control company to come out and set up traps to remove the termites and assign a one year service contract to the buyer. Mold usually will be very minor in scope and sometimes is as simple as take a spray bottle filled with bleach and spraying and scraping/washing the area in which the mold was found. Other times, it is hiring a mold remediation company to come out and provide their services and provide paperwork which will be presented to the buyer indicating that it has been taken care of. Regrading is something that sounds like having to totally change the structure of a property but it's just common language most inspectors put in inspection reports to pitch dirt away from a house to ensure when it rains the water runs away from the foundation. Replacing outlets might sound like having to totally redo all the electric in the home but it is far from that. It's a simple fix that usually costs around $100 per outlet to convert from a non-GFCI outlet to a GFCI code compliant outlet.

These conversations should be had with buyers up front as the above are common issues that should never be dealbreakers.

Now, what are some big issues that could pop-up and be make or break items? They fall into five buckets. Structural concerns, environmental hazards, code violations, major mechanical deficiencies, roof. Even if these issues do come forward during the home inspection, it is important that your client be made aware up front that any issues we discover, if major, we can always ask the seller to repair/provide a credit off the purchase price so that they can hire a professional to fix the issue to their liking. With that said, also reiterate to the client that the home inspection isn't just some sort of money grab where everything is fair game to ask for. We are going to be reasonable in what we ask for and not nitpick because when I eventually sell this house for you in the future I am going to demand the same from whoever your prospective buyer might be.

Structural concerns: These are issues related to the structural integrity of the home. Some issues I've seen in home inspections are cracks in foundation walls, settling, a rotted wood piling supporting a deck, a lally column in a basement that wasn't centered properly. These are issues that vary in degree of concern.

General settling is bound to happen. For example, this is common in back patios and older homes when they appear to have floors that are slightly slanted. This isn't that big of a deal. Cracks in foundation walls on the other hand, cause for concern. Before proceeding with the purchase, a structural engineer should be hired to come out to the property and give their opinion on what they think about the crack and if repair is required or can it easily be filled. A rotted wood piling supporting a deck will have to be replaced. It is probably best to request the current owner replace prior to closing rather than accepting a credit off the purchase price which they'll likely prefer. Last, lally columns aren't always centered on beams properly in basements and it's an issue that needs to be addressed. This is likely due to quick shotty work but nonetheless request that the seller repair this and provide receipts from a licensed contractor who performed the work. The last thing a buyer wants is to move into a house that is not structurally safe.

Environmental Hazards: The number one issue here and the one worth spending time discussing is older abandoned oil tanks and septic systems. Did the home ever use oil? Did they ever have a septic system before converting to the public sewer? The truth is, they may not know the answer to that as the property was there long before them. Therefore, it is important to encourage your clients to order a tank sweep along with their home inspection. If you are referring a good home inspection company, the inspector should be able to do this. The easiest way to explain a tank sweep is the inspector takes what equates to a metal detector around the property and sees if they get any hits that measure out to the shape of a tank. If they do, you will then have an exploratory dig to see if there is any tank in place. If there is, the tank will then be removed at the seller's expense and you will test the soil to confirm there is no contamination. If there is contamination the seller will have to remediate that and have it reported to the state department of environmental protection who will then only issue a, "no further action letter" once the soil is replaced with clean new soil and tests come back showing no more contamination.

Code Violations: These are as simple as the inspector pointing out something is not up to current construction code and putting it in their report at which time you alert the seller and they fix it. Common issues include no GFCI outlets around the sink/water sources, railings missing from stairs and a sump pump that is tied into a sewer line. All relatively minor but worth having the seller correct before closing. The biggest potential code violation that can be uncovered is that the seller did a bunch of updates in the home without taking out permits to do the work. Depending upon how long ago the work was done, what type of work was done and the quality of the work, the town could require the seller to actually rip out all the work and re-do it completely up to code. That would truly be a disastrous situation and one that could ultimately kill the deal.

Major Mechanical Deficiencies: This typically relates to heating and cooling systems in a home. It is important to let your clients know that just because the inspector states that the heating/cooling system is older and towards end of life expectancy that it is not grounds for asking the seller for a new heating/cooling system. Your clients will likely already know up front the age of the major mechanicals as most sellers will fill out a sellers disclosure form discussing the age and condition of these items, so the inspection is the time to confirm if the sellers representations were true or if there were some issues.

If during the inspection of the heating/cooling system, it is found that there is a leak, there are corroded pipes and there are other deficiencies, then it is totally fair game to ask for the seller to fix these or supply a credit off the price to compensate for the repairs necessary. Again, I just want to reiterate, if the inspector merely just says it is old and may need to be replaced in the next five years, that is not fair game to ask the sellers to install a new heating/cooling system.

Roof: Very similar to what we talked about with the major mechanicals section above. If a roof is found to be old and perhaps needing replacement within the next five years, this is not grounds for asking for a new roof. Now, if the roof is found to have holes, found to have shingles missing, found to have issues that could lead to mold or water intrusion then yes, it is fine to ask for these issues to be remedied.

As it relates to the above items, this is why it is imperative that you request a seller's disclosure form from the seller/seller's agent before submitting your offer. Let the seller's agent know that you are going to go over the seller's disclosure form with your client and take all the information enclosed therein into consideration when making your offer. This way you've now set expectations not only for your client, the buyer, but also for the listing agent. You've let the listing agent know as long as everything checks out on that seller's disclosure form, this will be a smooth easy transaction. However, if there are inconsistencies with that form and what shows up in the home inspection then there is a chance we may request repairs or credits.

The Buyer Consultation: You may be curious why I decided to put this as the last topic in this chapter rather than the first and the reason is because you can't have a proper buyer consultation without being educated on the previous items that we discussed. Once you've grasped the previous items, the buyer consultation process will be very simple and the most challenging part of it now will be simply finding clients.

The goal of the buyer consultation is two-fold. First, figure out what the buyer is looking for in a home. Second, build rapport with the buyer and lock them into a buyer's agency agreement by showing them the value of the services that you will provide. In total this whole appointment should only take 30-45 minutes.

When you first sit down, the first topic of conversation should be the discussion of whether or not they have already been pre-approved for a mortgage. You'd be shocked how many times buyers will respond with, "we haven't yet but we entered our numbers into a mortgage calculator we found online and we're confident we could afford a $600,000 home". The problem there is that the mortgage calculator likely didn't request them to submit pay stubs, tax returns, w2's, 1099's, pension statements or run numbers on debt to income and loan to value ratios. It is at this time that you should immediately tell them (not ask their permission to) you are going to put them in touch with your go-to mortgage broker who will be able to put together a full blown pre-approval for them. It's important to let them know that you're not doubting they can afford that $600,000 number they shared with you but rather that banks can sometimes be whacky and to avoid them wasting their time looking in a certain price point only to find out months later that a bank only has you pegged for $500,000, let's get it done up front. There is usually no push back on this.

Then it's time to start diving into what exactly they are looking for. I have found one of the easiest ways to do this is to go on your MLS site that you will be using and just copy the search criteria on there. After asking them about each item, follow up by saying, "is that a deal breaker". This way you can figure out which of their search parameters are musts and which are would like to haves. Below I have listed some of the top items I ask clients about.

Towns:

    Style of Home:
    Condition of Home:
    Bedrooms:
    Master Bedroom:
    Bathrooms:
    Square Footage:
    Schools:
    Basement:
    Finished Basement:
    Lot Size:
    Public Transportation Importance:
    Neighborhood or Busy Road:
    Heating/Cooling Preferences:
    Garage:
    Pool:
    Septic or Public Sewer:
    Natural Gas or Oil:
    Public Water or Well:

After getting all the answers to these questions. Tell them that you are going to send them five listings. Some might be currently available, some already accepted offers and some already sold. The purpose of this though is to ask them to look through the listings and provide their honest feedback on what they like and do not like about each home. Let them know these are not your homes so you will not be offended regardless of how harsh they want to be. In fact, encourage them to be as transparent as possible! Remember, the more you know about what they like and do not like, the less time they will waste in finding their dream home with you.

After knowing all this information, this will allow you to search for both homes that are on the market as well as homes that are off the market for them. You want to stress what you are going to do to find off market homes for them by both going door to door in areas that they want to be in as well as making cold calls. This is truly going over and above for the client. The reason you want to stress this is because of what you are going to ask them to commit to next.

It's at this time after you've gone through the buyer's consultation, laid out the scenarios, expectations and informed them about the, "team" that you will be setting up for them that you will lay the following request before them. "Mr. and Mrs. Buyer as I'm sure you know, this is a completely free service to you as the seller is the one who pays the commission if and only if we get to closing. My commitment to you is that I am going to provide you with the highest level of service possible and if at any time you feel that I am not meeting expectations please let me know as you are now my boss (say this with a smile on your face). The only thing that I ask in return is that you make a similar commitment to me in that you don't run around with other agents because any home you can see with them, I can show you as well so just let me know if you see something that sticks out and I'll get you all the information and schedule a time for us to see it. Sound fair?"

Not once in my lifetime has someone ever responded with, "that doesn't sound fair". Once they say that all sounds good, you will have them sign a buyers agency agreement with you and you can put language in that says that if they ever feel you're not meeting expectations they can cancel our agreement upon 48 hours notice.

Congratulation, you now know how to properly serve buyers. Now go do it.

Chapter 4

Dealing with Sellers

In real estate sales, sellers are the name of the game. Everything starts and ends with sellers and you can build an enormously successful business by dedicating your time and efforts to acquiring seller clients. From sellers come marketing opportunities, open house opportunities, excuses to go door to door and market property while getting in front of people, track record, referrals. I can go on and on but if you are properly servicing sellers, on average you should be able to obtain at least one buyer client for every listing that you take. In other words, two sales for one seller and that is not even counting the fact that you could very well be selling the seller their next home as well. Three sales for one listing? If handled properly, yes.

In chapter two we discussed prospecting at length, so by now you should know how to get in front of sellers. We will now turn our focus to how to properly turn that prospecting into listings acquired, properties sold, clients procured and most importantly, money in your pocket.

The Listing Appointment: After you've set the appointment to meet with the prospective seller, your goal now is to present to them your full array of services, explain to them how you are going to sell their property and ultimately close them. One of the best ways to ensure you have a successful listing appointment is to find out as much as you can about the homeowner's situation up front when prospecting or being put in touch with them. This entails asking them questions like, why are they considering moving, where do they plan on moving to, how soon are they planning to move, and if when you meet if they are comfortable and confident in your ability to get their home sold for top dollar are they willing to consider working with you. By doing this up front, you've set the expectation that you mean business and they shouldn't be surprised when you go in for the close when you do meet with them in person.

When you arrive at the prospective seller's house keep in mind that first impressions go a long way. Be friendly, be well dressed, smell good and be professional while striking the perfect balance with showing your human side as well. Be someone that your client feels as though they can open up to and tell anything. Let your client know that you believe your job is to provide them with all the necessary information to make an informed choice. Let them know that you are going to do everything in your power to get them the best offer possible and that sometimes the highest offer will not always be the best offer. Lastly, be sure to let them know that you have to sell their home not once, not twice but rather three times to the three B's. Buyers, brokers and the bank. We will talk more about the three B's in a little bit but first let's go step by step in this listing appointment.

Entering the Home: The first thing you want to do when you arrive is introduce yourself in person with a big smile on your face and let them know that you appreciate them welcoming you into their home. Pick out something in the main entry way or exterior to compliment them about and then tell them it is their turn to play the role of real estate agent and give you a tour around their home. During this initial walk-through ask them if it is okay if you take notes (bring a notepad, iPad, or take notes on your phone). You are doing this for two reasons. One, to actually take notes. Two, it is usually impressive and is a sign that you are detail oriented/organized and that is a good trait for someone who a homeowner may hire to sell what is likely their most valuable asset.

After you have completed the walk-through it is now time to sit down at the dining room or kitchen table and present what exactly it is that you are going to do to sell their home and why they should be hiring you for the job of getting that done.

I have always found that starting your presentation by showing homes that you have recently sold makes the presentation much easier and leaves sellers with far less questions. If you are a new agent, you may be reading this and thinking how can you do that if you haven't sold any homes yet? Simple, your best friend in your early days in your career will be the word, "we". "We recently just sold 123 Main Street, it was a 4 bedroom 2.5 bath colonial home. We listed it for $500,000 and after just one week on the market we received multiple offers and we sold it for $525,000." "We" could mean your team, "we" can mean your brokerage, in some cases "we" could just mean the real estate market that you participate in locally. Here is the truth, if a homeowner asks you how many homes you have recently sold and your response is, "well, none yet but trust me I know what I'm doing." You are going to have a very tough time getting the listing. So, recognize this and utilize the word, "we" to your advantage. Now, the questions in their head regarding whether or not you know what the hell you are doing are gone and the focus now becomes, what strategies and techniques you use to sell homes like theirs.

The strategies and techniques you use to sell homes are two-fold. Price the home right and make sure the house is in good present-able condition when it is on the market. There is a common phrase we talk about in the business, "no amount of marketing can sell an overpriced home". Say it again, "no amount of marketing can sell an overpriced home". It truly does not matter what you do to market a home if it is not priced right. Remember we must sell the home three times to the three B's. If we can't sell it to all three of them, we can't sell the house. We will get to the three B's in a little bit, I promise.

If we make the assumption that you are able to properly price the home (which we will discuss) then it becomes ensuring you get max exposure leading to obtaining top dollar for your client. How do you get max exposure? It is really a two-pronged approach. Active marketing and reactive marketing.

Active marketing would include things such as cold calling rental communities and seeing if anyone in those communities would be interested in buying. Sending out mailers to rental communities and people who currently have their homes on the market to make them aware of your listing. Going door to door in that neighborhood and asking people if they have any friends or family who might be interested in purchasing your listing (the, "just listed" script we talked about in chapter 2). Hosting open houses both public open houses for anyone in the public to attend and brokers open houses for all local brokers and agents to attend to preview the house for their client.

Reactive marketing would include different forms of online advertising. Most MLS services have a syndication feed where once the listing is submitted to the MLS it is then syndicated out to various other websites such as Zillow, Realtor.com and many others. Every agent will basically do this and it doesn't hurt to be transparent with a client and let them know that like every other agent you will be submitting their home to the MLS and that isn't anything that necessarily makes you different but just want to ensure you that I do that as well. Facebook ads are much more effective in my opinion as they allow you to directly target certain areas and interests or people.

When discussing anything you are doing that really differs from the competition, stress these items to your client. Make sure they understand that it is a value-added service and that you are going above and beyond and doing everything in your power to ensure we do not leave a penny on the table or a stone unturned. On the other end, if you are discussing certain things like hosting an open house or putting a home in the MLS, just be transparent and let your client know that these aren't things that make you different. By doing that, it will make the other strategies you are using that are different from your competition that much more powerful and impactful. If there is one thing homeowners appreciate from real estate agents, it is honesty. Sadly, there are a lot of dishonest Bullshitors in this business.

After you have gone through all the various things that you will do to get the home sold, it is now time to settle in on a listing price. This is arguably the hardest part of the presentation because naturally, most homeowners believe their home is worth more than what the realistic market value is. This is where we explain to them that we have to sell their home three times. We have to sell their home to the three B's. Buyers, brokers and most importantly the bank.

It is important to stress the three B's to clients because you need them to know that you are on their team and have their back. You do not want this to turn into them feeling like they're against you and fighting you on how much their home is worth but rather that together you are fighting the three B's. So, how do you explain the three B's to your clients?

Buyers: Quite obviously we must sell buyers on the home. This is accomplished from first and foremost simply getting them in the door through our marketing efforts. Second, by ensuring that the home is in tip top shape and that you could eat a whole meal off the floor if you please. Third, by reasonably pricing the home. After discussing the three B's, we will go over proper pricing strategy where we get the sellers to pick the list price without them even knowing they have picked their list price.

Brokers: These are our counterparts in the transactions. This is not a zero-sum game. There is such thing as creating a win-win situation for all parties involved and frankly it makes it a smoother and easier process when that is the case. Do not try to be a hard ass and demean them and go for their jugular. Remember, this isn't a one-time transaction. Your future in this business will be reliant on being a great agent to deal with as well over 95% of your listings sold will have the buyer brought by another agent.

Brokers know what the comparable home sales are, they know what the market value is and we have to be cognizant of that and explain that to the client when listing the home. The buyer could think it's a great home and you could have done a tremendous job in marketing the property but if they are working with a good agent, that agent will go through the comparable home sales with them before submitting an offer. Pricing is very important.

Bank: Of the three B's, this is the most important B that you have to sell the home to. You could have sold both the buyer and broker on the price, negotiated what you believed was a great deal, both the buyer and seller signed off, you went through the home inspection and everything came out clean. However, then the vaunted appraiser comes along on behalf of the bank and performs an appraisal. The reason the bank sends out an appraiser to the property is because they want to ensure the house that they are lending money on is actually worth what you are under contract for. Why does that matter, though? Well, here is the banks thought process. What happens if we lend the borrower money to purchase, they overpay for a house, they die suddenly and then we are forced to foreclose because the borrower is not making payments anymore. How are we going to get our money back? When explaining this B in particular, this is where you will really stress the importance of pricing the home right and go through a pricing exercise with the sellers.

Pricing the home right: As stated earlier, you never want to put yourself in a position where the homeowner believes that you are against them and trying to fight them on price. Remember, you want to position yourself being on their team and fighting common enemies, the three B's. When it comes time to discuss price, here is the best practice of settling in on a price where the seller picks the price without knowing they have even done so.

When you go to this home for the listing presentation, you should be bringing with you four comparable home sales. Two that are blatantly better than their home and then two that are similar or worse. Before laying these homes in front of homeowners you want to explain to them the point of why you are going through this exercise. Here is what I typically say. "Mr. and Mrs. Seller, here are four comparable home sales to yours. I have printed out all of the pictures of each listing and what I want to do now is to put ourselves in the shoes of buyers, brokers and banks as these are the four most likely homes they will look at when ultimately trying to determine the market value of your home. After looking through the pictures of these four homes, lets pretend we're in the shoes of a buyer and pick out which two we believe they would say are better than your home and why and also which two they would say are worse than your home and why."

The issue here sometimes is a seller will say that they believe their home is better than all four of those homes we put before them. In that case we will ask them instead, to rank them one through four and come up with reasons why a buyer might make a case for two of them being better and two of them being worse.

After the seller has laid out to you which two are better, and which two are worse, the most important thing to ask them is the reason why they believe that. This will be used to rationalize listing at a reasonable price. Easier said than done. See below for a role play example.

You: Mr. and Mrs. Seller, of the four homes we just looked through, if you had to pick, which two are better and which two are worse and why?

Sellers: 123 Main Street and 16 Park Street are better and we'd say 30 Godfrey Ave and 21 Plymouth Street are worse. We think we are better than 30 Godfrey and 21 Plymouth because we like our layout, finishes and updates better. 123 Main Street and 16 Park Street would probably be better because they have more updated kitchens, more updated bathrooms, finished basements, 2-car attached garages, and in particular 16 Park Street has a pretty cool enclosed trex deck with an outdoor bar.

You: Okay, that's fair. Here are the prices they sold for. 30 Godfrey sold for $425,000, 21 Plymouth sold for $430,000, 123 Main Street sold for $455,000 and 16 Park Street sold for $465,000. So would it be fair to say your home is worth somewhere between $430,000 and $455,000?

Of course it is fair to say that, they just said it to you! You essentially got them to price their home without them even knowing that they just priced their home! Now if they come back and say something along the lines of, "no that can't be, our landscaper told us we could easily get $500,000." (you'd be shocked how many times they tell you a landscaper, accountant, friend, neighbor told them a certain price and they believe that that therefore must be true). Then, you'd simply respond with, "Mr. and Mrs. Seller, the issue is that remember we have to sell your house three separate times. If we think about the bank in particular, they're going to look at 123 Main Street selling for $455,000 with a more updated kitchen, more updated bathroom, finished basement and a 2-car attached garage (you basically just repeat everything they said to you). Therefore, if we were to price right at even $455,000, we are shooting ourselves in the foot before we even start. Even if in this case we found one buyer to bid $455,000 we'd have no leverage in the transaction as it's not a price that would generate multiple bids so when the appraisal got done, if it came out at $435,000, the buyer would have every right to request we lower the price to $435,000 and if we didn't they could cancel the deal.

The best approach here is to price around market value at that $435,000 number and then possibly generate a bidding war where we have leverage and now can encourage a buyer to waive their appraisal contingency so if they bid $455,000, it is potentially now a solid $455,000. Doing this isn't being a snake, it isn't being deceitful, it is simply just doing what is in the client's best interest. There is an inverse correlation between days on market and sales price. In simpler terms, the longer a home sits on the market, the less and less it will sell for. It is in the client's best interest to price at a reasonable price and sell as quickly as possible as that will ensure that they receive true market value and perhaps even more for their property. As crazy as this sounds, the lower you price, the higher the house will sell for in most cases.

After you've done this and explained that you are still going to go above and beyond to get them the highest price possible, it is time to close. There are two ways in which you can close on them and get them to commit to working with you. One method is the hard close in which you say, "Mr. and Mrs. Seller are you comfortable and confident with my ability to sell your home for the highest price possible and meet all reasonable goals here?" I personally don't like this closing method as I often find the seller feels like they're being forced into something and don't feel comfortable. A lot of times they'll respond with, "Well, we want to talk things over first, can we get back to you?" This is where you'd respond with, "Mr. and Mrs. Seller, from my experience usually when a homeowner tells me they want to think about it and talk things over, it is because I didn't cover something I should have covered. What in particular do you want to discuss further?" Sometimes here they'll come back with the blunt truth which is almost always that they want to talk to other agents and get other opinions on price. At this time you should explain to them that realistically anyone can list a home for any price but that is the reason why we went through that exercise so that they could see what a buyer is looking at. As you imagine, the hard close greatly increases the chances of an awkward conversation and a tough ending to what should've been a great appointment.

The soft close is my go-to move. The soft close is saying something as simple as, "Mr. and Mrs. Seller, I am really looking forward to working together. The next step is for me to schedule my professional photographer to come out and take pictures and put together floorplans. What day would work best for him to come by, I can schedule him for Friday afternoon or would Saturday morning work better?" They'll respond with one of two answers usually. First, "Friday afternoon would probably work for us. Can he do 3pm?" Congrats, you just got the listing. They're not bringing your photographer out to just see what their house looks like. They're bringing the photographer because they are listing their home with you. They will sometimes respond with, "Well we don't know if we'll be able to have the house ready in time for the weekend for photos. Can we check back next week? We should have it prepped and ready by the end of next week." At which time you'll say, "Mr. and Mrs. Seller, let's do this. Let's tentatively schedule my photographer for the end of next week just so I can lock in a time with him. We'll schedule it for Friday at 4pm and if for some reason you're not ready, just give me a call the day before and I will re-schedule it. How does that sound?" They usually respond with, "That sounds good". Again, congrats, you just got the listing.

Closing is important. Closing is crucial. You can be great at everything leading up to that moment but if you can't close, you're not going to make it. I prefer the soft close, your preference is up to you.

Common Sellers Objections:

If it was easy, everyone would do it. The truth is, this isn't always the easiest business. Some of your most contentious moments will be the moments sitting down with a seller right before listing their home. Remember, they have a deep personal connection to their home. This is where they may have raised their kids, celebrated the holidays with loved ones, laughed, cried, put their personal touches on things. This home was the center piece of their life for the past 10, 20, 30, 40, sometimes 50 years! All of the aforementioned is to imply that they really value their home. They most likely value it much more than a random buyer off the street will and that's where we deal with our first and most common objection, price.

Price: We are not going to spend too much time talking about price here as we already went over dealing with how to price homes earlier in this chapter when we discussed stressing to sellers that we have to sell their home to the three B's. The strategy has already been put before you. What we will focus this section on is how to approach this situation and this conversation in a manner where the seller does not feel like you are against them but rather completely on their side fighting common enemies.

During this conversation it is important to keep in mind, what type of personality they have. Do they seem like the type that can deal with being shot straight or do they seem like the type who is emotional and needs to be eased into things? For example, for better or worse, I personally really lack emotions. There is almost nothing personal you can say about my home that could offend me. Other people are very emotional. Other people view their house as another member of their family. When you approach this type of person, you can't just lay out facts in front of them and think they will just take them at face value. You need to ease into the conversation and along the way continually compliment all the different aspects of their home worth complimenting, let them know that they've done a great job maintaining their home and that now you're joining forces to fight the three B's. In other words, for some people feelings matter more than facts and for others facts matter more than feelings. It is important to recognize what type of people you are dealing with.

The most common scenario you will probably find yourself dealing with is the, "we understand the comparable home sales and agree that based off those our house is probably worth $500,000 but wouldn't it be smart to start at $530,000 so we can leave ourselves some wiggle room and see if anyone will come up higher?". Everyone wants to get the most possible money for their home. The weird thing? Studies have shown that the closer to market value you price your home, the more it will ultimately close for. That is to say, if a home is worth $500,000 you should probably price it within 1%-2% of market value between $500,000-$510,000. That "wiggle room", number is typically 5%-10% above market value. This is a rather easy objection to deal with as we revert to the three B's once again. Here's how I typically deal with this.

Seller: "Kyle, we do understand the comparable home sales but we'd really like to start at a higher price of around $530,000 and see if we can get $530,000 and if we don't we can always lower the price".

Me: "Mr. and Mrs. Seller, I totally understand, and our goals and interests are directly aligned. I want to see us get the highest number possible. With that said we can realistically list at any number we want but we must keep in mind that we have to sell your home three separate times, to buyers, to brokers and most importantly to the bank. All the comparable home sales are showing in the $500,000 range so if we want to get $530,000 our best route would be to price right around $500,000 at fair market value and then get multiple bids and have a chance of getting someone to bid $530,000. In that scenario where we have all the leverage in the transaction, we can encourage buyers when making their final and best bid while competing against multiple offers to do things like waive either a portion or their entire appraisal contingency. This would mitigate the risk of not being able to sell to the bank. If we were to list at that $530,000 number, the odds of multiple bids is very slim and then when we get one bid, they are bidding against themselves and we have no leverage in the transaction and I've never seen a buyer waive a portion or their entire appraisal contingency when bidding against themselves".

Seller: "Well, besides that what would be the harm in pricing at $530,000? We could always lower the price later, right?".

Me: "The harm would be twofold. First, we greatly increase the chances of the house sitting on the market for an extended period of time. Now, I totally get that you are not in a position to fire sale this house and feel like you can wait and deal with it being on the market for a longer period of time but there is an inverse correlation between days on market and sales price. (I'd recommend bringing charts with you showing this. They are readily available online) The longer a house sits on the market it gets that stale feeling with buyers and they start asking themselves questions like, "why is that home still on the market? Why hasn't that home sold yet? Is there something wrong with that house? Why else wouldn't it have sold yet?". Buyers here also recognize they are going in and will be bidding against themselves giving them all the negotiating power. Second, if we do a price reduction that is just letting buyers know that we barely had any action, we recognize we were overpriced and at the moment we don't have any real interest in the property. Once again, it puts us in a poor position to negotiate as the reduction tells them all they need to know.

Commission: Depending upon the market that you wind up selling in, the standard rate of commission will differ. Due to anti-trust laws there is no universal set rate of commission, it is fully negotiable, but

I'd be lying if I told you there wasn't a standard rate. For example, in the markets that I sell in, that standard rate of commission is 5%. Some agents charge 6% and some agents charge 4%. Whether you want to call it an objection or not doesn't matter but the most common question you'll get about what you charge for commission is simply, "is that negotiable?". Here is how I deal with it.

Seller: Okay so what do you charge as commission?

Me: We charge 5% of the sales price. We do not charge any additional fees on top of that and we cover all the marketing expenses. Of that 5% we also split it evenly which is very important. 2.5% goes to the buyers agent and 2.5% goes to the sellers agent.

Seller: We heard there's agents that charge 4%. Why don't you charge 4%?

Me: Great question. The simplest answer as it relates to your interests is that charging you 5% is going to make you more money than if I charged you 4%. I know what you're thinking right now, so let me explain. As a buyer's agent, whether you bring a client to a listing paying 2% commission to buyer's agents or 2.5%-3% to buyer's agents, you are doing the same amount of work. In the MLS system on the agent side, before showing properties we get to see what the commission offering is to buyer's agents. When we see 3%, we really put in the extra effort to sell that home because on a $500,000 sale that would mean splitting $15,000 with our brokerage based on our commission split. If it was a 2% offering it would mean splitting $10,000 with our brokerage on a $500,000 sale. Both sales will require the same amount of work. It's kind of like if your boss told you at work that there was a promotion available. Both were to do the same exact job. One paid $100,000/year and the other paid $150,000/year, which would you chose?

Agents are no different than you. The truth is when showing that 2% offering they are probably going to go out of their way to point out the things that are wrong with the house in hopes of their buyer not wanting to buy it. With the 2.5%-3% offering, they will in this case try to point out what is right with the house and speak highly of it. I'm not making this up either, the stats back it up. Take a look at this data, (I actually have the data ready for the eight towns that I mostly sell in of the difference in sales to list price ratio between listings offering less than 2.5% commission to buyers agents vs listings offering 2.5% or more to buyers agents) homes that offer 2.5% or more to buyers agents on average sell for 98% of list price. Homes that offer less than 2.5% to buyers agents on average sell for just 86% of list price! So while a seller may think they're saving 1% on commission, they are really net effectively losing 11% on the sale. Does this make sense?

The above is how you should handle that situation. Facts matter. As we say, men lie, women lie, numbers don't lie. Let the numbers and data tell your story.

We want to sit down with other agents: Sometimes sellers feel obligated to sit down with at least three agents before determining who they are going to list with. Throughout your presentation you should keep this in mind and subtly mention some of the bullshit you know other agents will bring up. For example, when talking about price I always make sure to mention that it is a very common strategy for agents to tell sellers an unrealistically high price to secure a listing because then they lock owners into a six month listing agreement and know they'll be able to beat them down on the price all while hosting open houses every weekend and meeting more buyers who they'll sell every home but the listing they met them at. It would also be a good idea to ask the seller if there was anything you didn't cover that they'd like you to touch on. I usually say something along the lines of, "Mr. and Mrs. Seller, thank you for giving me the opportunity to sit down with you and interview for the job of selling your home. I greatly appreciate it. Usually when a homeowner tells me they want to still meet with other agents it's because I wasn't thorough enough in my presentation and I probably missed some things that didn't give them the confidence in me to make a commitment. If you had to name just one thing you'd like me to elaborate more on what would it be?". I find this to be powerful as it shows I am making an attempt to close on them and I usually follow up by letting them know that I am not trying to be pushy but just keep in mind that similarly if I sense a buyer has interest in their home I am going to try to strike the iron while it is hot and get them to commit to their home rather than walk away and wait a few days and have second thoughts. Remember, you want to position everything as being beneficial for them when working with you.

Remember, acquiring seller leads is the name of the game. The more sellers you work with, the more buyers you will meet, the more marketing opportunities you will have, the bigger track record you will create and ultimately, the more homes you will sell.

Chapter 5

Marketing The Property

No amount of marketing can sell an overpriced home. Your best form of marketing is simply pricing the house in line with comparable home sales. Due to the three B's it doesn't matter what you do to market the home if it is overpriced. This chapter is going to be a lot shorter than you probably anticipate and it's for good reason. I really want to stress to you how much pricing matters. Marketing is completely irrelevant unless you are priced reasonable. To recap how to properly price houses go back to chapter 4 where we talk about pricing.

Here is a little secret in our business that everyone knows but doesn't like to admit. The difference between a top agent and an average agent selling a home is probably only a 1%-3% difference in sales price. On a $500,000 home sale that is a difference between $5,000-$15,000 so it's not exactly peanuts either. Below we will list some of the top ways in which you can market a home that will achieve you that 1%-3% bump in sales price. Remember, be honest with sellers, even go as far as explaining this to them. Why? Because if you tell a seller you're going to get 10% more for their home than another agent, you're being a bullshitor and it's very obvious. But if you're honest and explain to them that a top agent like yourself who is actively marketing properties will get them 1%-3% more than an average agent they'll not only take you more seriously but they will also recognize that you're concerned about getting every last penny out of the sale for them.

Here is how that conversation typically goes with me.

Agent: Mr. and Mrs. Seller, the majority of buyers who will come to see your home are going to come see it whether I list it or another agent lists it because both of us will put your home in the MLS, on Zillow and on Realtor.com. So, if you're looking in Roseland already and a home hits the market that's of your interest, you will look at it whether it's listed by me or John Smith from ABC Realty. Does that make sense?

Seller: Yes

Agent: So my goal here is to expand your buyer pool beyond the people who will be automatically looking at your home anyway. I want to ideally put us in a position to have leverage when negotiating whether it be because we have multiple bids or because we have a bunch of interest generated in the first week or two of the home being on the market. Here are some of the ways in which I do that.

It is at this time that I will go over some of the strategies I use to market properties actively to unconventional or out of town buyers. I will list these below.

1. Renters: A great pool of people in which you can market property to is local renters. The question is, how do you find them? It's a lot simpler than you'd think. Just simply look up the rental communities and buildings locally and then through Mojosells.com map out the community to pull the phone numbers to call those people. You can also send them postcards directly to their home as well.

   One of the big reasons why renters rent is because they don't think they have enough saved up for a down payment. This is where it is beneficial to have some base knowledge of mortgages such as the FHA loan program which allows borrowers to take out a loan with as low as 3.5% down.

2. Move-up Buyers: Move-up buyers come in two forms. Buyers who are moving up in size and staying within town and buyers who are moving into a new town because it is more prestigious and has better schools for their children. The traditional move-up buyer who is just getting a larger home will most likely see the home whether you list it or John Smith from XYZ Realty does. However, the other move-up buyer might not even be aware of what the particular town your listing is in has to offer. They might not realize the school rankings, the extra curricular activities offered, the proximity to public transportation, the main street entertainment close by. When targeting this type of buyer the first thing you do is sell the town and then once they are sold on the town, you sell them on the house.

A big piece of the above strategy is first finding out what are the towns that people are traditionally moving from. For example, I sell a lot of homes in Roseland, NJ. In Roseland we have a lot of move-up buyers who come from five specific towns. Clifton, Nutley, Bloomfield, Belleville and West Orange. So, when I have a Roseland listing, I am targeting people in those towns who are either in higher priced rentals or people who currently have their homes on the market. If they have their homes on the market, they are obviously moving and if they're move-up buyers I want to make sure they are aware of what Roseland has to offer them and what the house I have listed does as well.

3. First-Time Buyers: Obviously if they're first-time buyers that means they are currently renting. However, depending upon the market that you are in, these buyers could be near but in some cases they can be far. We discussed targeting local renters under #1 but what about renters who are currently living in urban areas who are looking to now move out to the suburbs? For example, I primarily operate out of the North Jersey suburbs. There are a good chunk of first-time buyers who come out to us from the NYC, Hoboken and Jersey City markets. Luckily for me, the rental buildings are plentiful in those areas and by no means hidden. Therefore, when I list a home in North Caldwell, I will target these buildings by simply calling the residents and simply asking them if by any chance they are considering moving out to the suburbs. Sometimes it's an older couple who will basically curse me off, other times it's a young

couple who just got married who is looking to move out to the suburbs.

4. Delayed Showing Strategy: Every listing that I take, I list on a Wednesday but do a delayed showing until Sunday. This means that it appears online and across all platforms on Wednesday but we do not allow any showings until Sunday. The reason for this is, it gives me 4 days to actively market the property and drive a ton of traffic to the open house. Anyone who wanted to see it Wednesday-Saturday will come to the open house Sunday which I will hold for a maximum of two hours. The reason for this is, regardless of how long you host the open house for, the same amount of people will come. It's a better look and will show there's more interest if you have 20 couples come in two hours than 20 couples in four hours. It will give off the vibe of there being a ton of interest and if a buyer likes it that they will have to come in fast and they will have to come in strong. This increases your chances of not only a strong offer but also multiple offers therefore causing the home to sell for above asking and give you all the power at the negotiating table!

5. Staging the Home: Selling a messy, smelly home is tough. If you were to take two identical homes side by side, one is staged and prepped and the other is a disaster with junk all over the place and it smells like farts and cigarettes, the difference in price will be drastic. As an agent you should always make recommendations as to how different rooms should be laid out and encourage decluttering. It's also a

good idea to have a home stager on file who you can refer to clients. Home staging is truly a worthwhile investment. If a homeowner can spend $5,000 on staging and it gets them $20,000 more for their home is that worthwhile? Of course it is! Where else can you find that type of return on investment in a 2-3 month timeframe? No where! You should always sell home staging to them as an investment rather than an expense and give the same, "return on investment" talk to them as I said above.

6. Professional Photos: Not much to say here. Have a professional photographer do your photos for every listing. Almost all home searches start online and first impressions are everything. They typically charge no more than $150 for photos as well. This isn't optional, this is a must if you're serious about this business.

If you take one thing away from this chapter it should be that your best form of marketing is by simply just pricing the house properly. If you don't price the house correctly, the rest of the chapter is irrelevant as the house will not sell.

Chapter 6

Negotiation

There are two parties involved in every sales transaction, a buyer and a seller. It should be pretty obvious that they have completely and totally different interests at hand. The buyer wants to get the home for the lowest price possible and the seller wants to sell for the highest price possible. In this chapter we will discuss negotiating strategies when on the buyer's side of the table and likewise on the sellers side of the table. But first, lets discuss the different types of negotiating scenarios.

Scenario #1, The Traditional Negotiation: The traditional negotiation implies that it is not a multiple bid type of situation and the buyer and seller are negotiating one on one. Keep in mind, this doesn't mean that another buyer can't come in while you're trying to negotiate and make a separate offer as well.

Scenario #2, The Bidding War: This negotiation will be a little more complex as there could be anywhere from 2-20 bids on the property and as a buyer you will have to put forth the BEST offer to win, not necessarily the highest. We will discuss what this looks like. Below we will start off talking about being a seller in both situations and then afterwards we discuss being in the shoes of a buyer.

Seller in a traditional negotiation: After being on the market for two or more weeks and not accepting an offer, it is at this point where the pendulum swings to the buyer's side. The buyer now knows they won't be getting involved in a bidding war and that they have some power here. This is where it becomes increasingly important that you have priced the home well and that you have comparable home sales to substantiate that claim. From my experience, a lot of buyer's agents will just submit offers at a certain percentage below list price and just take a, "lets see what happens", type of approach. It's important that you not get testy with this agent but rather come from a position of facts and data and express the desire that you'd love to work together and make a deal happen.

When the buyer's agent submits their offer, if you believe it's way off what the comparable home sales show, simply ask them how they came up with the number. Tonality is so important here. You don't want to come off like a snob with your tonality implying they don't know what they're talking about. Instead ask genuinely, "Hey Joe, received your offer on 123 Main Street, thank you very much. I want to present it to my clients with comparable home sales as I'd love to work together. Can you let me know which comps you used to come up with your offer?".

If the agent comes back and says he didn't have any specific comparable sales he used then you know he's just throwing an offer out there and taking the, "we'll see what happens approach". It's at this time where you can pull the best possible comps you can find to make the case on your client's behalf that their home is worth $X. If the agent comes back and says he used three specific comparable home sales then it's up to you to look at those comps and see if they are fair comparisons and if so, show them to your client when presenting the offer so your client knows the perspective at which the buyer is coming from. When you ultimately counter when trying to get a higher offer out of the buyers, you should go back with your own set of comps to sell the story of the higher price and how you can rationalize it. Remember, facts and data matter. When presenting an offer backed by facts and data there will be no ill will and it will come off as genuinely trying to work out a fair deal.

Keep in mind that there could be other contributing factors besides price that can be negotiated as well. These would include things like closing date, language around the appraisal, home inspection and down payment amount. We discussed all of these individually in chapter 3.

Seller in a Bidding War: Ideally you will have put yourself in position to generate multiple bids on your seller's property putting your side in the driver seat and in full control. Here is where you want to exploit your leverage and ensure your client is getting the highest and more importantly best offer as possible. As discussed earlier, I highly recommend listing all homes on Wednesday's and doing a delayed showing until Sunday. This will allow the handling of your multiple bid situations to be smoother, easier and more standardized. Let's say you begin showings on Sunday, it would be a good idea to allow for at least 4-5 days of showings. So if on Sunday after the open house an agent calls you and indicates that their client would like to make an offer, let them know that showings just began today so you are going to allow at least four days worth of showings and if before Thursday at least one other offer comes in that you will set a final and best date for Thursday at 5pm. Communicate with them that you will be in touch throughout the week to keep them up to date on offer count and if anything changes.

Let's make the assumption here that three other parties indicate they'll be submitting an offer prior to Thursday. It is at this time that you will go back to all the buyer's agents and let them know final and best offers are set for Thursday at 5pm and what exactly would be some good ways to have offers stand out. Below are the four main factors that can really have an offer stand out.

1. Price- no explanation needed

2. Language about Home Inspection: Guide them here let them know an example of what good language would look like. Keep in mind, buyers will never completely waive the entire inspection but they usually in bidding wars are comfortable with the following type of language, "Buyer will waive all inspection items totaling less than $2500 for a single item". In other words, they're not going to nitpick you on little things that may pop up.

3. Language about Bank Appraisal: Buyer's rarely completely waive the appraisal contingency because if they do that would mean if they were under contract for $500,000 and the appraisal came out at $450,000, they're promising to put down an extra $50,000 in cash to make up that gap. So, guide them and recommend language such as, "In the case

of an appraisal short fall buyer is willing to make up the gap between appraised value and sales price by up to $10,000.".". This would mean if they bid $500,000 and the appraisal came out to $485,000, they're not going to ask us to lower to $485,000 but rather just to $495,000.

4. No Home Sale Contingency: Ask that the buyers not make their offer contingent upon selling any real estate.

The above will put your seller in the strongest possible position and likewise put you in position to ensure you've utilized your leverage and created a great experience for the seller which will hopefully come back to you in the future with an abundance of referrals!

Buyer in Traditional Negotiation: The traditional negotiation begins after the home has been on the market for about 2-3 weeks as discussed above. Let's now tackle it from the buyer's perspective. First and foremost, as a professional real estate agent you never want to approach any negotiation from the, "hey, lets just see what happens", perspective. You want to always be able to rationalize your offer and how you came up with your number. While representing the buyer, you obviously want to make the case for the lowest number possible. Therefore, if you are essentially negotiating against yourself find the lowest possible sale that a case can ever be made for as being a comparable. This would mean if your client was offering on a home that was moderately upgraded, use a comp that is similar bedrooms, bathrooms, style, square footage but just a little underwhelming upgrade wise. Remember, when negotiating, the sellers list price for the most part means nothing, comps mean everything.

When a seller tries to say something like, "well, we were listed at $600k and we've already countered at $590k, so we've come down $10k already, you need to come up more". This is a very weak move by a seller's agent because the seller's agent should know that the list price means nothing. Hypothetically they could have listed that house at $6,000,000, if they countered at $600k would that have meant that you already got $5,400,000 off the price? Of course not. So, if they try to pull that card just combat it with showing your comps and mentioning that hypothetically the house could have been listed at any number, right?

What other cards do you have up your sleeve when you can't settle on price? There's a few obvious ones that we have mentioned previously. Those include language about the home inspection, appraisal, closing date and no home sale contingencies. In this situation you're the only bid on the table so you should only use these additional strategies if there's a real stalemate in the negotiations and your client does not want to move up in price but is okay with foregoing some minor things on the inspection because they are handy as an example.

Buyer in Bidding War: Being on the buyer's side in a bidding war can be tough because all rationality is thrown out the window. In bidding wars, the house will almost always sell for more than what the comps can substantiate. If you're working with a first-time home buyer or a first time in a long time buyer, they will most likely have to get outbid on a number of bidding wars before they realize that, yes, houses do often selling for more than the asking price. If you don't set proper expectations for buyer's up front and communicate with them that they should expect to pay above asking price for any house that has a bidding war, then they'll feel ambushed and caught off-guard when you advise them that in order to win the bid, they have to offer above asking. Here is how I typically approach these situations.

Agent: Mr. and Mrs. Buyer, the listing agent has informed me that they have five total offers and are calling for final and best offers on Thursday.

Buyer: Okay, so what does this mean for us?

Agent: As previously discussed this inevitably means the house will sell for above asking. How much above asking? There is no way to tell as the listing agent will just inform us how many offers they have coming in but they will not disclose how much those offers come in at.

Buyer: Well, we don't want to overpay for the house.

Agent: Of course not and I'll never force you to do anything you're not comfortable with. So, let's first look through the comparable home sales. The sellers are listed at $500,000 but there are comparable home sales that can rationalize up to $525,000. With that said, the four other buyers that we are competing with are most likely being shown the same comps and they'll easily be able to rationalize offering $525,000 as well and from my experience what I usually see here is there will be one offer that stands out above that. So, the determination you have to make is what number would this house have to go for, for you not to be mad that you lost out on it?

Buyer: If we offer $525,000 would that get it done?

Agent: It's really impossible for me to predict as we never know what the other offers will be. I get that you're probably thinking right now that this answer doesn't help you but I'm just being very straight forward with you about this. These type of multiple bid situations are extremely unpredictable. For example, I don't want to tell you to offer $530,000 and that will get it done but then we get a call from the listing agent saying they went with another offer and six weeks later we see it closed for $535,000 and you think to yourself, "Kyle lost us that house, we would've paid $535,000 and he told us $530,000". This is why I always tell my clients what the comps rationalize and then ask them what number would this house have to sell for, for you not to feel you lost out on it.

Buyer: Okay, we will have to think about that.

Agent: Here is the good news, they call it highest and best offer for a reason. The highest bid doesn't always necessarily win but rather the best offer does. There's a few ways that you can still win this without being the highest offer. We can put language in the offer about limiting the home inspection only to items totaling more than $2,500 for a single item. This will comfort them that we are not going to nitpick them on little things and try to take a ton of money off the price that we agreed to. We can put language in there about the appraisal that says in the case the appraisal comes out lower than the proposed sales price we will make up the difference up to $10,000. This will comfort them that if we bid $525,000 and the appraisal comes out as low as $515,000 we won't ask them to lower the price. Lastly, this isn't always a huge deal breaker but we can let them pick the closing date as long as it's 45-90 days after offer and acceptance.

Your job is to supply the client with as much information as possible and then empower them to make the decision. When you do this, they always feel as though you have their best interests at heart. Remember, nothing is worse than when someone feels as though they've been caught off guard or they are left feeling stupid. By educating your clients and arming them with this information you've empowered your client to feel fully confident and okay with the outcome regardless of who the seller chooses.

Above I called the bidding wars, "negotiations" but the truth is there really is not much negotiating going on. It's more or less strategy. It's you as the seller's agent telling the buyers what you're looking for, or you as the buyer's agent putting your best foot forward and seeing if the seller chooses your offer. Strategy and approach is the key here and it all starts with arming your client with information.

Chapter 7

Making Clients for Life

I hope we are all approaching this business with the future in mind. We don't want to just churn 'em and burn 'em. Every client that we work with, we want to turn into a client for life. A client who when they have friends and family looking to buy/sell/invest in real estate, the only name that comes to mind is yours because of the great experience they had when working with you. As real estate professionals, we are in the experience business, not the sales business. The sooner you recognize this, the quicker you will be on your way to building a consistent, high volume real estate business that feels as if it is perpetually running itself. The obvious way to make clients for life is by providing them with top notch services all around. In other words, to do a lot of what we already focused on in prior chapters. This chapter will be dedicated primarily to post-closing and how to maintain that relationship while building what we like to call, "raving fans".

As previously discussed, it's important that during the transaction you recognize the fact that you are a human and your client is a human. What I mean by this is that it doesn't always have to be business, business, business. People do business with and refer people who they know, like and trust. Develop a relationship with your clients. You should always want your clients to feel as though they know you, they like you and most importantly they trust you. Besides finding out what is important about their home search, inquire into what is important to them as people. What are their interests? What are they passionate about? What do they do for work? Once you find out what they do for work, ALWAYS ask them what does their ideal client/customer look like? Let them know if you come across anyone that could use their services you'd love to reciprocate and refer them business. I cannot express how powerful that last bit is. Now, not only have you serviced them with a high degree of care but you're also looking for ways to further help them. How do you think they'll feel after all of this? Heck, they may just immediately run to Facebook and post about how great you are! At least people like my mom would but that's another story.

Here are some of the strategies I use to create clients for life post-closing.

1. The Referral- The referral is a strategy that we just discussed but it's worth going over again. You're doing this genuinely because you appreciate the fact that this person just trusted you to represent them in what is most likely the single largest financial transaction of their lifetime. The approach to this is a simple conversation. I usually use the following line, "Hey Joe, let me ask you something. What does your ideal client or customer look like at your job? I'm just asking because I want to be able to refer you some

business should I come across anyone that you could help".
It's really that simple and then the conversation opens up.
This shows that you truly are not just in it for a one-time
transaction. This instead proves that you not only want to
maintain this relationship but be able to refer each other
business. I can't express how powerful this is.

2. The Quirky Anniversary Card- You want to do things that
   really make you stand out. One of the tactics I have used
   that I've found effective is tracking all of my buyers closing
   dates and on those dates years later send them an anniversary card. It'll be a simple card that says something along
   the lines of, "Joe and Jane, happy anniversary! 1/15/2021
   officially marks the four-year anniversary of you closing on
   123 Main Street. I hope your home has brought you much
   happiness and joy over these four years and will continue
   to do so for the next 40!". It's just another way to stay in
   front of past clients and in the card you never once mention
   or ask them to refer you business but ultimately those are
   things that will come from this.

3. The Holiday Drop-Off: Around the holidays every year I
   drop off a bottle of wine or apple pies to clients. I usually do
   this between Thanksgiving and Christmas. It's just a simple pop-by and drop off of an apple pie. I never even alert
   them to when I am coming. I simply show up and ring the
   doorbell with an apple pie in hand. You constantly want to
   have interactions with past clients. Don't make the mistake
   of making this seem like a business visit by leaving your
   business card. Handwrite a nice card and sign it.

4. Client Appreciation Parties: These can come in many forms. These can come in the form of a dinner party, a huge tailgate and outing at a baseball game/football game, or just your classic backyard barbeque. Whatever the event is, make it fun and make it social. Remember we are in the experience business.

5. Random Texts: I know, doesn't exactly sound like a legitimate strategy but it is. This is just being a human being and texting someone out of the blue about something you think they'd be interested in. If your client is a huge sports fan and their favorite team does something (good or bad), shoot them a text about it and jump into a conversation. If your client is a foodie and you just tried a new local restaurant or a new dish at a local restaurant, text them about it. If your client has a child that plays on a local high school sports team and you see they did something impressive text them about it. Trust me, if there's one thing parents care about more than breathing, it's their kids. Any time they have an opportunity to talk about their kids, they will. Give them the floor!

6. Annual Market Valuation Update: Whether people are looking to sell next year or never, your past clients are almost always at least curious as to what their home is worth. The most effective way to do this is to not give them a specific number but rather once a year send them the three most comparable homes to theirs that have sold nearby. It often will result in them calling or texting you and asking what that would all mean for their homes valuation.

7. Become Friends on Social Media: This is a delicate one. If you're the type that posts like wildfire on social media and you post some relatively controversial stuff, probably a good idea to steer away from this. However, if you're the type to post mostly funny stuff and pictures just a couple times a week, it will be a great idea to befriend them on social media. This will allow them to see the personal side of you. You should always post some real estate related content once or twice a month as well to ensure that side of you is staying in front of people. The best type of content is videos of market updates.

8. Make Education Videos About Real Estate Investing: There are so many people who want to invest in real estate but just don't know where to start or what to do. Arm your past clients with this knowledge! Not only are you helping them, they may just take the leap and buy an investment property through you which means another sale! A true win-win scenario. The returns generated from real estate investments beat the crap out of alternative investments. If you can inform your clients about this not only will they be intrigued and perhaps buy an investment property, they will pass the information along to friends of theirs who will want to work with you as well! We will talk at length about multi-family investment real estate in the following chapters.

I want to keep this simple and just give you some ideas. The eight above I feel are great strategies that you can implement to ensure that you have created a sustainable business that generates perpetual referrals. Most importantly for any of the eight above tactics to prove effective, you will first have to service the client properly during the transaction. If you don't, you can throw all of the above out the window.

Chapter 8

Analyzing Multi-Family Investment Properties

Real Estate has created more millionaires than any asset class in the history of humankind. The power of leverage, the tax benefits and how investment properties are evaluated makes it a truly unique and special asset class. It is important to arm yourself with this knowledge not only for your clients but also for yourself. In this chapter we will discuss how to evaluate investment properties, how to see where the value can be captured and learning how to put together a plan when buying an investment property. Before we dive into those, let's go over some basic terminology that will be needed when dealing with investment properties.

Capitalization Rate: This is another way of saying your yield the property would generate if you were to buy it 100% all cash. To figure out your "Cap Rate" you simply take your net operating income divided by your sales price. For example, if the net operating income the property generated was $10,000 and it sold for $200,000 then the cap rate would be 5% as $10,000/$200,000 is 5%. This formula can also be used in another order once you know the cap rate in a market. If you're going to list an investment property and you know the net operating income is $20,000 and the cap rate in the market is 5% then NOI/Cap Rate = Value. When talking with agents or investors about this term always use the term, "cap rate". That is the common jargon in the business.

Net Operating Income: This is taking the gross income minus the operating expenses (not including the principal and interest expense from the mortgage). For example, if the gross income the property generated was $20,000 and the operating expenses were $9,000 then your NOI (net operating income) would be $11,000. When talking with agents or investors about this always use the term, "NOI". That is the common jargon in the business.

Gross Income: This is all the revenue the property generates. Examples would be rents, laundry, parking, utility bill back, as well as other things on larger properties such as common space rentals, vending machines, etc.

You might be wondering how you can look up the cap rate in a particular market and unfortunately there's no direct answer to that. You will have to do your own research by going through the MLS and looking at recent sales of 2-4 family homes and seeing what cap rates they went for. On these listings, the listing agents will always advertise NOI and then the sales price will be posted when it sells. So simply all you will have to do is take the NOI divided by the sales price and you'll find the cap rate. Don't just do it for one property though, do it for a bunch of them so you can see what the average cap rate happens to be. As an example, let's just say a few properties have NOI's of $10,000 and sales prices of $200,000, then the cap rate is probably about 5% in that market.

Here is another thing to keep in mind, most agents have no idea how to properly calculate NOI. Therefore, you should be very skeptical of the NOI that they are advertising. ALWAYS ask the agent what is included in the NOI number. Is it just rents minus taxes and insurance? Or are the operating expenses all truly accounted for? Operating expenses should include things such as property taxes, insurance, maintenance, property managers fee (typically 5-10% of gross collectible income on 2-4 family properties), water/sewer and in some cases things like heat and hot water if it's an all bills paid property. That last term sounds complicated but all it simply means is that the units aren't separately metered and therefore the tenants heat and hot water is included in rent. There could obviously be more operating expenses, but these are the bare minimum that should be accounted for.

Let's begin the fun part now. Evaluating the property, finding the value aka the meat on the bone and putting together a business plan.

1. Evaluating Investment Properties: Finding the fair market value is straightforward as we discussed above in the cap rate formula. However, the return profile that investors look for isn't solely revolving around cap rate. It is largely driven by what is commonly referred to as, "cash on cash" return.

   A cash on cash return is a calculation determining what your return profile will be based on the amount of cash that came out of your pocket that you invested. For example, if you were to buy a $500,000 property with a cap rate of

7%, that would mean the property generates $35,000 in NOI annually before paying your mortgage. On a $400,000 mortgage that would cost about $24,000/year. This would mean that your cashflow left over after you pay all your operating expenses and mortgage is $11,000. Considering that you put down $100,000 then your cash on cash yield would be 11% in year one. This number is just simply to calculate what your yield on your money invested will be annually. Cash on Cash= Free Cashflow/Cash Invested.

2. Finding The Value: What we mean by this is what is the value-add business opportunity? Where is the meat on the bone? Do the comps show that if we do things like install vinyl plank floors, resurface old countertops, put in a backsplash, new kitchen appliance package, brush nickel hardware on the cabinets, new vanity in the bathroom and reglazing tubs that this will add $200 per unit to the monthly rents? What if doing all of those things costs $7500? Well, you might think adding $200/monthly rent is only an extra $2400/year and therefore you'd have to hold the property for over three years for it to pay for itself. Well, that is certainly not the case because of how investment properties are evaluated.

Let's say for example you have a 2-family property and the units are each 2 bedrooms and 1 bathroom and their rents are $1500/unit. If the nearby comparable rentals have all the upgrades that we previously mentioned and rent for $1750/month than it would be a no-brainer to spend $7500/unit in renovations to raise rents by $200/unit/month to conservatively raise rents to $1700/month. If you were able to raise rent on each unit by $200/month that would be a total of $400/month and over the course of a year that would be an extra $4800 in net operating income. If we assume a 5% cap rate in that market then $4800/5% would produce an increase in value of $96,000! So, you spent $15,000 on renovations and it raised the value of the property by $96,000. This is an absolute no-brainer!

When sitting down with a client and looking for potential value-add opportunities, keep in mind to calculate how the renovations you are proposing will effect the market value of the property. All you would have to do is take the increase in NOI and divide that by the cap rate. It's something you could do on your phone right inside the house while showing it.

3. Business Plan: The profit is made when you buy, not when you sell. Plan your work and work your plan. When buying an investment property for a value-add opportunity, what value are you going to add? We previously talked about a lot of ideas under #2. Those included installing vinyl plank floors, resurfacing old countertops, putting in a backsplash, new kitchen appliance packages, brush nickel hardware on the cabinets, new vanities in the bathroom and reglazing tubs. Sometimes the opportunity might just be improving the curb appeal with new masonry, new landscaping, re-siding, new windows or a fresh paint job. On the other end of things, the value-add opportunity could simply be just becoming more operationally efficient and lowering

expenses. Perhaps the landlord is currently paying for water and sewer and therefore they go through with some sort of water conservation by installing low flow toilets and low flow showering heads therefore on a 4-family lowering the water expenses by $1,000/year and at a 5% cap rate that raises the value by $20,000! The value is everywhere you just have to look for it and point out the opportunities to your clients and then run the numbers. The numbers will tell the whole story and do the selling for you! Just remember, all you have to do is calculate how much your renovation will affect the NOI and just divide that by the cap rate and that will tell you what the increase in value is!

4. FHA House Hack: Whether you yourself want to get into real estate investing or friends, clients want to, the number one most productive and efficient way this can be done is through the FHA house hack. House hacking is a slang term used in the real estate investment world to describe buying for example a 4-family and living in one unit while renting out the other three. Maybe you're thinking, why would someone want to do this? The reason is simple. Leverage. Through a house hack strategy since you are living at the property you can typically use an FHA loan to purchase with as low as 3.5% down and use the other three units of which you won't live in as income when applying for your loan. Typically, the lender will take 75% of the other units rent rolls as long as their leases are not month to month and they have at least 3 months of term left on the lease post-closing.

With all the above valuation strategies in mind and ways in which to capture that value-add meat on the bone, here would be your ideal scenario. Let's say that you are going to buy a 4-family home for $500,000 and live in one unit and rent out the others. Ideally, you'd want to buy one that has some upside that can be captured through doing light value-add renovations in the amount of $7,500/unit. Let's assume that by doing $7,500/unit in interior value-add you are able to install vinyl plank floors, resurface old counters, put brush nickel hardware on the cabinets, paint the cabinets, new kitchen appliance package, put in a backsplash in the kitchen, swap in a new vanity in the bathroom, reglaze the tubs and paint the interior walls with a fresh coat of paint. And yes, $7500 is more than enough budget to do those things.

There are four units and let's assume they are all 2 bedrooms and 1 bath and rent for $1500/month. Unit 1 is where the current owner lives and you will move into that unit. Unit 2's lease ends three months down the road, unit 3's lease ends six months down the road, and unit 4's lease ends in nine months. After closing, you move into unit 1 and before you physically move in, you do the above for $7500. When unit 2's lease ends in three months you offer them a new lease at $1750/month for their current unit or they can move into your fully updated unit 1 for $1750/month. The idea here is you are trying to raise the NOI and ideally you want them out of unit 2 so you can update it. If they choose to stay in unit 2, they are going to pay a rent premium as if the unit was updated, so ideally you hope that they choose to move into unit 1. To sweeten the pot you can offer them two movers to help move their stuff one door over. These, "movers" can be hired off the task rabbit app for probably no more than $500 total for the day. We'll explain why this all makes sense in a moment. Now, once you move into unit 2, you do the same exact upgrades you did in unit 1 for $7500. If lined up properly those updates should take no more than 48 hours to complete. Three months later unit 3's lease comes up at which time you tell them they can stay in unit 3 not updated for $1750/month or move into your unit 2 for $1750 fully updated and you'll offer them two movers to help move all their furniture. Regardless of whether they choose to move into unit 2 for $1750/month, stay in unit #3 at $1750 (while not upgraded) or leave, you win. Let's assume they leave. Then you would put unit 3 for rent at the new price of $1750 after you've spent your $7500 updating it and you get a new tenant in place. Lastly, three months later unit 4's lease comes up at which time you repeat the process we discussed previously. And let's assume they decide to move into my fully updated unit 2 for $1750, while I move into unit 4 and spend $7500 updating it.

In the above example what I have done in a years' time is raise the NOI on the property by $12,000/year. I took the rents from $1500/month to $1750/month making an additional $1,000/month or $12,000/year. If we are in a market that has 5% cap rates, what we've done is created $240,000 in value as a NOI of $12,000 divided by a cap rate of 5% is

$240,000! I bought this $500,000 property with only 3.5% down, then went on to spend $30,000 in upgrades and for that $30,000 investment in upgrades I was able to generate $240,000 in value! Do you see how valuable the house hack can be! This is a monster strategy for wealth creation that I encourage everyone to look into not only for themselves but for their clients, friends and family as well. Make videos explaining this to them. Simple videos, they don't need to be more than five minutes in length. I have about a five-minute-long video going over this on my YouTube™ page that I send to any prospective investor clients. It is powerful!

The beauty of the above strategy is if properly executed this person will become a real estate addict and will likely look to sell that one within a year and do it again on another property. Can you blame them? While working their regular job they just made about $200,000 in additional income which they may not even need to pay taxes on at time of sale if they sell it through a 1031 tax-deferred exchange. I'm not going to get too far into that in this book but do yourself a favor and look up 1031 exchanges. They essentially allow you to sell one investment property and buy another within six months and defer the tax burden off to a later period of time. There are a bunch of rules in 1031 exchanges such as how soon you must identify the property, who has to hold onto the money, if you touch any money you have to pay taxes on it, along with a laundry list of others. It's something worth learning about.

Chapter 9

Looking For Subdivision Opportunities

Subdivisions are simply taking one parcel of land and chopping into multiple parcels. These can be great opportunities for yourself or for clients who are looking to flip who you are looking to build strong relationships with. There is no better way to build a strong relationship in business than making somebody a whole lot of money and this is a great vehicle to do so.

So, how do you even find subdivision opportunities? It's a lot simpler than it sounds. If you're ever driving through a neighborhood and just see a big empty lot it means one of two things. It is either a single lot that hasn't been built on that is owned by someone or it is a side yard of one of the adjacent properties and it may just be a great candidate to split into two separate lots. In an ideal world it is a side yard and a prime subdivision opportunity.

To get your hands on one of these opportunities is as simple as when you spot it, knock on the two neighboring properties doors. When they answer the door just ask them, "Hey, by any chance do you know who owns that lot". If they tell you someone else owns it and it's a totally separate lot than it is not a subdivision opportunity. If they tell you either they themselves or the neighbor owns it then it is 100% a subdivision opportunity and if that's the case, ask them if by any chance they'd consider subdividing or selling off the entire property including the house they are currently in. To be blunt about it, 99/100 times, they're going to tell you they're not interested but this is a pure and simple numbers game because the money that can be made on these opportunities are huge. Here is an example below of a subdivision that I personally executed.

The neighborhood in which I had grown up in had a property that had an enormous side yard. I'm talking half a football field deep. I lived on that street from first grade to fourth grade. Every day after school me and all the kids in the neighborhood would congregate at my house and play every sport under the sun on the dead end and this yard. Street hockey, basketball, football, whiffle ball, you name it and we played it.

As I grew older and got into real estate I wondered to myself, why didn't the owners of that house ever subdivide and sell off the side yard as a separate lot? I had found out that the nice woman who lived there had passed away and her son inherited the property. It was empty for a couple years and I had reached out to him to see what his intentions were with the property and he told me that he'd be selling it in the next year or so. Some time went by and one day he called me and said he'd like to meet me at the property to discuss selling it. I met with him at the property and the first thing I advised him to do was subdivide it and then I could sell off the house and lot separately and ideally get him more money. Now, there was no guarantee the subdivision would get approved and it could drag out only to fail but I felt it was worthwhile pursuing. He told me he didn't want to pursue that and just wanted to sell. At this time I told him, I would be interested in just buying it off him directly and therefore in a private sale, no commissions would be involved creating a win-win situation for both of us.

We wound up settling on a purchase price of $410,000 for the 100x160 lot which had a 4-bedroom home on one half of the property and the other half was just a large empty side yard. My intent here was to split the property into two separate lots that would be 50x160 each. There were about 32 lots on this street in total and even after splitting them, a 50x160 lot would be the third biggest lot on the street so I felt this was a slam dunk. I had also consulted a local engineer, who was regularly hired for subdivisions, to get his opinion on my plan and he indicated he was very confident it'd be approved so that was very encouraging. It was now time to assemble the subdivision team.

Team Members for Subdivision Application:

1. Engineer: The engineer will be putting together the site plans and how everything will be placed and built. I'd be lying if I told you I knew all the little terminology of every single little thing they do but that is why you hire them. The best way to find the right engineer to hire is go through the town's meeting minutes and see who the engineer is who is constantly proposing subdivision applications in town. This engineer clearly is good at their job but maybe even more importantly they know exactly what the town is looking for

from applicants. This will speed up the process and limit the total numbers of times you will have to go before the town. This will also save you money in billable hours.

2. Land Use Attorney: You should ask the engineer who they recommend you hire as a land use attorney. The reason is because they will be the ones going to battle for you before the town and it's always best when they get along and have worked together before. The attorney will also be the one making the case for you.

3. Public Planner: This one is not always necessary but it certainly doesn't hurt. The public planner will usually be recommended by the land use attorney if need be. A public planner is a professional who specializes in putting together plans for towns in regards to design/uses in certain areas. Their role if needed in this process is to provide their professional opinion that what we are proposing fits in like a glove with the towns planning and zoning goals.

After you've assembled the all-star team then it is game on. This team will tell you exactly what you need to do to get your proposal approved. They are the professionals, shut your mouth and listen to what they say (the Jersey in me just really came out). After they've put together their proposal and feel it's bullet proof they will then get in front of the board in town to present. This will be a meeting that is open to the public and the public is even given the floor to express their opinions and concerns if they have any objections. Your attorney is required to send out what is called a 200-foot list prior to this meeting. In other words, they must send certified letters to all neighbors within 200 feet of the property notifying them of when and where the public meeting will be and what is being proposed. This is where things get fun.

At the night of the public meeting, show up and shut up. Let your engineer, attorney and planner do all the talking. Remember, you know nothing. They know everything. The more you talk the less you win. Therefore, we just let the neighbors stand up, complain, act crazy and embarrass themselves. In other words, you let them bury themselves. Your team has prepared for what standard objections will be fired their way and they are prepared and ready to bury them. They will complain about things such as building another house will push water onto their property which is not the case since seepage pits will be installed. They will complain that they just don't like the idea. They will complain that it won't look right. To be frank about it, they'll be grasping at straws. If you have a solid plan in place, they will fail miserably and it'll be entertaining to watch. DO NOT make any facial expressions when they are being fools. DO NOT smirk, DO NOT shake your head, DO NOT make any sudden movements. Just sit there with a blank look on your face. After the board approves it you can glance with a little smile at them and maybe even wink but before that time do not do anything.

You probably read the above and felt some emotion. Well, yeah. The thing is most neighbors who come to these meetings come because they have nothing better to do and just like to hear themselves speak. If I'm proposing to build a brand-new house next to you that will most likely be the most expensive house on the block, all it is going to do is raise your value, you DOLT!

Getting back to my above example, the subdivision application was successful and we got approved. I chopped the lots into two separate 50x160 lots. I spent about $110,000 in renovations on the current house and sold that for $600,000 and wound up just getting the plans for the new 50x160 lot and selling the lot with the plans for $225,000. This whole process took about six months in total. Below are what the profits on a deal like this looks like. I rounded the numbers to make them even.

Expenses:

Purchase Price: $410,000

Subdivision Process and Construction Plans: $15,000

Carrying Costs (taxes, insurance, financing): $15,000

Renovations on Current Home: $110,000

Closing Costs and Buyers Agent's Commissions on Sales: $25,000

Sold:

Current Home: $600,000

Lot: $225,000

Total Expenses: $575,000

Profit: $250,000

One last thing to point out. You may be curious why as a real estate agent I had to pay out commissions to buyer's agents and not just sell myself. The answer is simple. Well over 90% of all buyers work with real estate agents so why would I want to sell for sale by owner and eliminate 90% of my buyer's pool? It'd be foolish. Yes, I know how to sell homes but more important than that is having people to sell the homes to. I'll gladly pay out that commission because it's going to net me more money in my pocket at the end of the day. That objection we talked about in earlier chapters with for sale by owner's being foolish isn't just something I preach, it's something I genuinely know is factually true and therefore I practice it.

Chapter 10

Passively Investing in Real Estate Syndications

This was the game changer for me. When I came across real estate syndications and learned about them I felt as though I just found the end of the rainbow and the pot of gold. It was everything I was looking for. Through syndications you can invest passively as a limited partner and just hand your money over to someone buying an apartment complex and do zero work and truly have your money work for you rather than you working for your money. On top of this it will pay you annual cashflow and it will throw off massive tax deductions through depreciation all while your capital is appreciating along with the property. Sounds too good to be true, right? It's only too good to be true if you invest with the wrong people.

We will focus this chapter on discussing what to look for in a syndication from both a macro and micro level. At the time of writing this book I have invested in 12 multi-family syndications and have invested millions of my own personal capital into them. In this chapter we will also discuss some of the tax benefits. Keep in mind the tax code is ever changing and by the time you read this book the tax code could have been revised. I am also not a tax professional or financial professional so this should not be construed as tax planning or financial advice and I advise you to consult with your tax or financial professional to see how your individual situation would apply in your case.

First and foremost, let's define what a syndication is in layman's terms. A syndication is a partnership on steroids. It is basically an exceptionally large partnership where you might have three general partners go out and search for an apartment complex to buy. They find one they like, they make an offer, it gets accepted, they front the costs on due diligence, inspections, and loan application fees. After everything checks out and they decide to proceed, they then reach out to their investors and essentially sell off shares to join the syndicate.

But what should you be considering before handing your money over? What are the selling points of a syndication? What are the returns like? What makes a good syndication? What makes a bad syndication? What is a good market? What is a bad market? What makes a good sponsor? What makes a bad sponsor? How do I even find these opportunities? We will talk about all of the above and more.

Where To Find Syndication Opportunities:

- People. People put together syndications. The key is meeting the right people. There are great websites like BiggerPockets. com where you can ask for recommendations of multi-family syndicators that people have invested with.

- Referrals: Seek out people who have invested in syndications before and have had a good experience with a sponsor. This could be as simple as posting on Facebook, "Has anyone ever invested in a multi-family syndication?".

- Multi-Family Syndication Conferences: There are big multi-family syndication events all throughout the country where sometimes thousands of syndicators show up along with passive investors. At these events ideally you want to seek out passive investors and just ask each one, "can you share with me 2 sponsors you've invested with that you'd invest with again?" Ask as many people this question as you can. Eventually you're going to find the same name popping up time and time again, that is a sponsor who you should look to contact and get on their investor list so when they have a deal they're looking for investors for, you can hop right on in.

I also personally put together syndications with partners for properties in Texas and Phoenix. If you'd like to be added to my investor list, feel free to email KovatsMultiFamily@Gmail.com. Most of our syndications require a minimum investment of $75,000.

Macro Criteria: Before even beginning to think about investing in syndications, make sure the sponsors that you have met are doing syndications in areas that you want to invest in. So, from a macro standpoint, what makes a good market?

- Population Growth: The more people coming into the area the better. You want to have positive net population growth in the market you will be investing in. This isn't rocket science. The more people there are, the larger the renter pool, the higher the demand and as long as new supply does not outpace population growth you're in a good area. Usually if population is soaring in an area that also means it's a desirable area from both a quality of life and economic standpoint.

- Employment Growth: Is employment plentiful in the surrounding area? Are there businesses relocating and forming in the area where your prospective new tenants can be employed? If they don't have jobs, it'll be hard to pay rent. Follow the money.

- Wage Growth: What does the data on wage growth say in the area? This will reflect how much you can raise your rents on a property. If wages are stagnant or declining your property may not be able to grow income.

- Rent Growth: What has year over year rent growth in the area been? Anything lower than 2% should leave you a little skeptical.

- Diversity of Employment: By this we mean a lot of different types of sectors and industries. We don't want to be in a market where there is only one sector or employer. If that's the case, then if that sector does poorly or that employer shuts down, you're done.

- Landlord/Business Friendly States and Localities: This is arguably the most important of the above. You can have an area that meets all of the above criteria's but if they're not landlord friendly it could be a troublesome scenario. You want to be invested in what we call, "don't pay, don't stay states". In other words, you don't want tons of loopholes that can be exposed by tenants to enable them to stay in an apartment for months on end without paying any rent. What I'm about to say is not a political statement but merely a matter of fact as a general rule of thumb. Republican run states and areas will be more business and landlord friendly and democrat run states and areas will tend to be less business and landlord friendly. It's not to say that there are not democrat run areas that are nice and meet some of the above criteria, it's just that there are a lot more straight forward common sense laws in republican run areas. As an example, at the time of writing this book, I live in New Jersey. I do not have a single penny invested in NJ real estate, while I have millions invested in Texas.

Micro Criteria:

- Neighborhood Data: What does the data say on the neighborhood from a variety of perspectives.

- Median Household Income: I want to find what the median household income is in that census tract which can be found on the US census website.

- Where do People Work: I want to know what type of jobs our prospective tenants hold, and I want to know where they are working.

- Proximity to Supermarket: How close is the property to a supermarket? This one is super important to me because I invest in blue collar workforce housing where often the family only has one car so properties near supermarkets are always big winners as it allows the tenants the ability to walk to the supermarket.

- Crime Data: There are various websites in which you can look up what the local crime is like in an area. Shoplifting nearby obviously isn't a big deal. However, if there were multiple murders in the past year within a few block radius, I wouldn't invest.

- Proximity to Parks: If the property is nearby a park or borders a park it's almost like having a free amenity for your tenants. In one of our most recent acquisitions, we bought a 265-unit property in Dallas which shared a property line with a public park. This was tremendous because also nearby was a school so this was really attractive to families with kids. Families with kids often stay longer which means less turnover and more collectible income.

- Proximity to Schools: The closer to schools the better as there is not always bussing available.

- School Rankings: Having a good public school district is always great as across the board, parents do typically want to be able to provide their kids with a good education.

Sponsor Criteria: Who are the sponsors putting together the deal? The sponsors are the general partners. They are the ones who went out, sourced the deal, offered, did the due diligence, did the inspections, everything came back in good shape and now they're seeking investors to passively invest. They need passive investors/limited partners for the deal to work. For example, if they were buying a $25,000,000 apartment complex it might require $10,000,000 in equity up front for down payment plus capital reserves and things of that sort. They most likely don't just have $10,000,000 laying around and therefore they sell share to investors.

The sponsors should have some kind of track record. It'd be ideal if you know someone who has previously invested with them in other deals so you can pick their brains on what the experience has been as an investor with them. Even more so, it always helps if you get to personally know the sponsors too. Do you know them? Do you like them? Do you most importantly, trust them?

Here are the simple key questions I ask sponsors before investing with them for the first time.

1. How many syndications have you been a GP (general partner) on?

2. What were your two most recent syndications?

3. Can I see the most recently monthly financials on those two most recent syndications along with recordings of your webinars from when you were raising capital for them? This is key because it's basically them putting their money where their mouth is. It's almost as if you watch their old webinars while having a crystal ball to see into the future to see if they actually performed as they pitched they would. If they did perform exactly as they projected or even better, then that is pretty damn powerful.

4. What % of your total return on syndications that you've gone full cycle on came from cap rate compression than NOI growth? I ask this because I want to see if they were a classic example of a rising tide raising all ships or if they were an operational savant. I prefer the latter as that will stand the test of time.

Returns: Depending upon the syndication that you invest in there are typically two types of return structures. They will typically be structured as a straight equity split or a preferred return.

Straight Equity Split: This very commonly will be and 80/20 split. Meaning that 80% of all of the cash flow, appreciation, depreciation for tax purposes will be paid out and allocated to the limited partners and the other 20% will be paid out to the general partners. At time of sale the 80/20 split should not kick in until the LP's get all of their initial capital invested returned to them and after that has occurred the rest is to be split 80/20. This split is simplistic and straight forward.

Preferred Return: A preferred return will mean that the LP's are due the first certain % of return and after receiving it then the rest of the cashflow or appreciation will be split based on the equity split. Here's an example, "8% preferred return and then 70/30 thereafter". This would mean that annually the LP's are due an 8% return on their money and if they don't receive that then it accrues and builds up to be paid at a later time. For example, if you invested $100,000 in that aforementioned example and in year one you received just $6,000 back in cash flow then the GP would've accrued an additional $2,000 that is owed to you next year to catch up and get even or to be paid at disposition. So, if in year two of that deal you got paid out $10,000 in cash flow then they'd be even with your account. However, if in year two they once again only paid out $6,000 in cashflow then they would've fallen further behind therefore making it likely that you'll be caught up on your arrears at disposition, aka when the property is sold. The benefit of this is that the sponsor doesn't get paid anything more than an asset management fee until you earn 8% annually, so it should in theory motivate them to perform. To just give one more scenario regarding the deal previously mentioned. If you invested that $100,000 and it was an 8% preferred return and then 70/30 thereafter if the property sells in exactly three years, you would have to get $24,000 in total back before that 70/30 split kicks in for the remaining sales proceeds.

Sometimes these deals are set up in what is called a waterfall structure. What that means is that once the GP's hit a certain target, let's say 13% IRR, then the 70/30 split turns to 50/50 for the remaining left over sale proceeds thereafter. There are a bunch of different ways in which waterfall structures can be set up and they will certainly be confusing when you first hear about them. I suggest going on YouTube™ and looking up videos explaining waterfall structures before investing in a deal that has one. It'll much better help you understand them.

Conservative Underwriting: You want to ensure that the assumptions and projections that the deal sponsors are making are reasonable and conservative. I'd rather them under promise and over deliver than over promise and under deliver. Below are factors that I'd keep a real close eye on to see if they're being overly aggressive.

- Is the exit cap rate raised by AT LEAST .1% for every year of the projected hold? The reason this is important is because when cap rates compress (drop) then values go up. A great way to inflate the return is by the sponsor projecting a low cap rate at time of disposition. While that very well could happen, it should be a bonus, rather than being expected.

- Are the property taxes being raised from what they currently are to what they will be after purchase? In most states property taxes will raise significantly after purchase. It's important that this is accounted for. For example, if it's a 250-unit property and you projected after acquisition that property taxes stay the same when in fact they go from $250,000 to $300,000, then if the cap rate in that market is 5% that is a difference in market value of $1,000,000! $50,000 / 5% = $1,000,000. That is literally a $1,000,000 mistake. You don't want this to happen.

- Unrealistic Rent Bumps: Rent bumps of anything above 10% are typically cause for concern to me. I don't mean 10% after doing renovations, I'm talking about 10% of organic rent growth. My concern is, does the market call for it? The easiest way to research this is simply go on websites like apartments. com and look at nearby properties and see what their units look like and what they are charging for rent. Then put yourself in the shoes of a tenant and think if given both options which would you choose? Ideally you don't want to invest in a property that will be the market leader in rents.

- Vacancy Projections: This comes in two forms. Typically referred to as economic occupancy and physical occupancy.

Economic occupancy is what % of units are occupied by paying tenants. For example, if you had 100 units and 95 were occupied but only 90 were currently paying, you would have a physically occupancy of 95% but an economic occupancy of 90%. You want to ensure that if you're investing in a deal where over the first one to two years there will be renovations then that should be reflected in the occupancy projections. If you see them projecting occupancy to remain the same throughout the 5-year hold then there is most likely a bunch of other things that they didn't account for in their underwriting and this should be a red flag.

- Sensitivity Analysis: Every deal should have a sensitivity analysis. This is running different scenarios to see what the returns and financial position of the property would look like if this were to occur. These scenarios are often based on figuring out what your breakeven occupancy would have to be to meet all bills, debts and obligations. In other words, I think it's a good idea to see what the best case, worst case and most likely case will be.

- Loan: I personally am not a fan of bridge debt. Bridge debt or a bridge loan is a form of short-term financing. I am not a fan because at maturity if there cannot be an extension and the GP has not hit their numbers or can't find a buyer they may default and lose the property causing you to lose a lot of money or all of your money. I prefer a deal with long-term debt on it. Ideally a 10+ year fixed rate loan and if it's a variable rate, I can get on board with that as well as long as they've purchased a rate cap which is essentially capping the max interest that may be charged.

- Budget For Contingency Reserves: I want to make sure that the GP's aren't just raising money for their ideal scenario, I also want to ensure that they are raising equity for reserves in case some things pop up that they weren't expecting. For example, a heating/cooling system breaking and needing to be replaced is a very common unexpected (but should be expected if that makes sense) expense.

Questions I ask Deal Sponsors: On top of scrutinizing the above, what are some good questions to ask deal sponsors before investing in their deals? Ideally, they cover most of these in their webinar presentation but in the case they do not, it's worthwhile asking them the following questions.

- Are you putting any of your own personal capital into this deal? I want to know that they have skin in the game.

- Bridge Loan or Fixed-Rate Debt?

- Will there be an acquisition fee? Acquisition fees are very common. An acquisition fee is typically between 1-2% of purchase price. Now, if the sponsor has an unbelievable track record of success, it may be warranted. However, if it is a newer sponsor it may not be. At any rate anything higher than 1% I believe is a little aggressive. Think about it this way. If a syndication group was buying a $40,000,000 apartment complex and charges a 2% acquisition fee then they've essentially bought it for $40,800,000 as $800,000 will be paid from the investors to the sponsors at closing. So even if that deal completely tanks, the moment they close they've already made $800,000. I'm not the type that complains about people making wheel barrels of money (trust me) but rather my concern here is are they still motivated? Are our interests aligned?

- Is there a disposition fee? This is essentially a commission paid out to them when the property sells. This one rubs me the wrong way too because their reward should be the equity split if they've performed.

- What is the asset management fee? An asset management is a fee paid to the sponsors for managing the asset, dealing with investor communications, and basically making sure the ship is being steered in the right direction. In my opinion asset management fees should always be a % of the effective gross revenue the property generates rather than the amount of equity invested in the deal. The latter never made much sense to me, but you see that commonly with institutional private equity firms.

Preferred return or straight equity split?

- At the time of sale, do I get all my initial capital invested returned to me before the sponsors get a penny? I want to make sure our interests are aligned and a great way to showcase that is for me to get all of my initial capital invested back before they touch any money at time of sale. In other words, if I don't get my initial capital invested back, they make no money. This should be motivation enough to perform.

- Have you personally secret shopped the comparable properties? I want to know why you believe the comps make a good case for this deal.

- What is the number one concern you have about this deal? If they say nothing, then they're full of shit. Every deal has concerns. I just want to know what concerns do you have and if it is related to older mechanicals like heating and cooling systems were those accounted for in the reserves?

- How did you come up with your property tax projections in the pro-forma? Was it a guess? Did you consult a tax firm? Did you consult your property management company who ideally is managing properties nearby? What's the worst-case scenario for property taxes?

- Does the property management company have experience in the area and with this class of property? I want a property management company that is already in the area as they would have all the vendors on file for when something needs to get done. Also, if I'm invested in a C-Class deal, I don't want a management company who primarily handles A-Class properties, it simply won't be a fit.

- Does your insurance policy cover loss of rental income in case of a fire and does your insurance policy cover the FULL cost to rebuild in the case that 5 or 25 units are damaged by fire? This is important. I was invested on a deal where a fire ripped through one of the 13 or so buildings on the property. It took about 18 months to rebuild. Luckily, the sponsor had insurance for things such as, debris removal, loss of income, code upgrade and replacement cost insurance. Had they not had this that would've been a disaster.

- What upside does this deal have that you haven't mentioned? I'm not going to hold you to it, I just want to know. This is a good one as you'll be surprised how many sponsors hold back on mentioning some of the additional upside of the deal. The reason they do that is they're conservative and would rather under promise and over deliver and that is a great thing.

- Are your personal friends you've known your whole life or family members investing in this deal? I know sounds a little personal but it's a great question. Why? Guess who people really don't want to screw over and lose money? Their lifelong friends and family.

- What is your exit strategy, in particular how will you position the sale of the property to have additional upside for the next purchaser? What type of meat will you leave on the bone and how will you prove proof of concept? For example, one of the properties we own was all 2 bedroom/1 bath or 3 bedroom/1 bath units when we purchased. It was 120 units and on five of the three-bedrooms we added a half bathroom. Those units receive $75 rent bumps for that ($900 in additional NOI a year). It cost us about $4,500 per unit to do that. At a 5.5% cap rate (which is what is in that market) that is an increase in value of $16,363. $900 / 5.5% = $16,363. So, when we go to sell, we will share these numbers with prospective buyers and let them know there are 115 more units they can do that on. We've shown proof of concept, it actually works. So $4500 x 115 = \$517,500 to add the half baths on the other 115 units and at a rent bump of \$75/month or \$900/year that will result in an increase in value of \$1,881,818! It's a great selling point.

- The last point and I just want to stress this one again. The most important part to me here is the person. I always like to say I invest in people, not properties. Do I know, like and trust the GP's? Are they genuine people? Are they in this for money or for value? I can't stress how much more important the people are than the property. If you find good people to invest with, the rest takes care of itself. There are GP's out there that I trust to such a degree that if they tell me they have a deal tomorrow I'd simply say count me in as a passive investor. You'll get to that point too.

Tax Benefits: The tax benefits are enormous. The tax benefits almost always ensure that your cashflow distributed to you will be tax-free that year as you should have enough depreciation on your K-1 to offset any cashflow distributed. A K-1 is a tax document that you get every year when you invest in a syndication indicating what your taxable gain or perhaps what your "loss" is for the year. Due to cost segregation studies that accelerate depreciation, it is very common that not only will tax not be due on your cashflow for the duration of the hold but also, you'll have additional deductions from depreciation left over that can be used against your income if you're a full-time real estate professional.

If you recall the presidential elections in 2016 and 2020 there was a lot made of the fact that Donald Trump didn't pay any federal income taxes. As a real estate professional, this was a foregone conclusion to me. To the media, they made it seem like he was some kind criminal for doing such. The truth is 99% of people and those in media have no idea how taxes work and the fact is that 98% of the tax code shows you ways to lower your tax burden. Focus on the 98%, not the 2%. I highly recommend reading, *Tax Free Wealth 2nd Edition by Tom Wheelwright.* It will open your eyes and help you keep more money in your pocket for you and your family because remember, it's not about how much money you make but rather it's about how much money you keep.

Once I learned the tax code and started heavily investing into real estate, it provided me with enormous deductions that significantly cut my federal income tax burden. For some people, well in fact for a lot of real estate professionals, it will take their federal income tax burden down to $0. For example, on average for every $100,000 I invest in a syndication, in year one I get a K-1 back with a loss showing around $75,000 due to depreciation. This is paper loss. It doesn't mean I actually lost any money out of pocket. If you're a full-time real estate professional this can be used as a tax deduction against your income and perhaps take your federal income tax burden down to zero. As always this depends on your particular financial situation and this should not be construed as tax advice, please consult a tax professional to learn more about this.

My Ideal Realistic Deal: Throughout this chapter I have laid out my criteria for what I want in a syndication that I'm investing in so you should have a good idea of what that looks like at this point in time. I'm going to stress a particular point once more though, invest in people not properties. Once you find good syndicators who you know, like and trust the rest takes care of itself.

Now, for me personally from a number's standpoint, I am more of a cashflow investor than a speculative investor. For that reason, syndication wise I stay away from development/new construction projects. This is not to say they're bad to invest in but rather that it just doesn't mesh with what I'm looking for. I'm a pretty conservative investor and therefore my ideal realistic deal meets the following numbers:

Cash Flow: 7.5+ cash on cash annual return

Average Annualized Return: 15%+

Economic Occupancy: Over 90% on the T-12 (trailing 12 months financials)

Ideally, I would also like to see close to 50% of the projected total return over a 5-year hold period coming from cash flow. The reason for this is cash flow is rather predictable whereas appreciation really isn't. Cash flow is in the hands of the GP's from a management standpoint in their ability to drive revenue and being operationally efficient to lower expenses. Appreciation recognized at time of sale is very time and market dependent, something that is out of their control.

The 15% average annualized return is a conservative return too. Every single deal I have invested in that has gone full cycle and sold, the average annualized return has been higher than that. It beats the hell out of the returns the stock market provides. Think about what a 15% average annualized return means to you and your family. It is estimated that from 1957 forward, the S&P 500 has produced an average annual return of around 8%. In real estate you will more than double that from a post-tax return perspective due to the tax benefits derived from depreciation. However, let's take the time to go through an example now. Go on google and type in, "moneychimp compound interest calculator". Now do two examples. A stock market example of investing $100,000 with zero annual addition and 30 years to grow at an 8% interest rate and then do a real estate example investing $100,000 with zero annual addition and 30 years to grow at a 15% interest rate. You will find in the stock market example that $100,000 will turn into $1,006,265 in 30 years time. In the real estate example, you will see that $100,000 turn into $6,621,177 in 30 years time. Remember, I've written this book primarily for those below the age of 30. Let's say hypothetically you want to leave a legacy, you want to make sure generations and generations below you are taken care of for eternity and therefore, you've made a commitment to not touch that $100,000 for 50 years until you're 80 years old. Now run those numbers based off 50 years. You'll find $100,000 invested in the stock market for 50 years at 8% interest will turn into $4,690,161. Ready for the real estate example? $100,000 invested in multi-family real estate for 50 years at 15% interest will turn into $108,365,744.

This is the power of real estate. This is the power of leveraged returns. This is why real estate has created more millionaires than any asset class on earth. Don't have $100,000 to invest right now? Good. You just read this book. This entire book was designed to get you to this point. To the point where you've become such a good real estate salesperson that you have the money to do things like this. What could you do with $100,000,000? Not $100,000 but rather $100,000,000? One little hint, gucci belts and cars ain't it. Do something good for the world and for people. If your drive is materialistic, you'll never get to this point anyway.

Remember, a journey of a thousand miles begins with one single step. Luckily for you, your journey of a lifetime is about to start with a single action. So, it is now time to put this book down and, screw it, just do it.

ABOUT THE AUTHOR

Kyle Kovats is a real estate professional based out of New Jersey. He got his real estate license fresh out of high school while at Rutgers University. Since beginning as a real estate agent, Kyle has served as a leasing agent, sales agent, flipper as well as both a passive investor and general partner in real estate syndications.

In 2016 Kyle was recognized by the National Association of Realtors when he was named to their annual 30 under 30 list recognizing some of the top professionals in the industry nationwide under the age of 30.

Kyle is also the owner and lead instructor at Kovats Real Estate School in Northern New Jersey.